이 근상 목사님 혜존

김학랑 올림

2004. 4. 24.

항상 건강하세요.

Winning Campaign Strategies
Methodologies and In-Depth Guide

Hak Ryang Kim(Ph.D.)

Camst, Inc.
Columbus, Ohio

Camst, Inc.
2936 North West Blvd. Upper Arlington, OH 43221
23026 Paseo De Terrado #4 Diamond Bar, CA 91765
homepage : http://www.icamst.com
e-mail : camst@icamst.com

Library of Congress Cataloging in Publication Data

CIP Data to come

ISBN 0-9748516-0-4

10 9 8 7 6 5 4 3 2 1

Contents

Tables

Figures

Preface

In my professional experience as a campaign strategist in the last decade, I have seen that a winner in an election is certainly different from a loser. The winner campaigns on the basis of the principle of scientific campaign strategies, while the loser usually does not have any knowledge of campaign strategies. Furthermore, the winner usually prepares his/her campaign strategy early, so that he/she runs a well-planned out campaign.

Thus, I always suggest that a new candidate must study and learn the core principles of campaign strategies before deciding to run, and experienced candidates would be better off reviewing the principles of campaign strategies one more time before they launch a campaign.

The purpose of this book is to make a candidate the winner by conveying the principles of campaign strategies to him/her. Campaign strategies can be roughly divided into three steps: *accurately predicting what happens in the process of a campaign, making careful plans based on the prediction,* and *executing the plan well.* This book guides candidates in taking these three steps by offering a balanced composite of theories and the experiences that I gained in working as a consultant in numerous campaigns.

I learned much about campaign theories when I did my graduate work in Political Science at The Iowa State University in Ames, The University of Iowa in Iowa City, and The Ohio State University in Columbus. In my doctoral dissertation, *The Adaptive Change to the Electoral Defeat: The Conservative Party in Post War Britain*, I offer a comprehensive review of some theories related to campaign activities.

After completing my Ph.D., I became actively involved in assisting and consulting for the campaigns of various politicians in Korea. I helped numerous candidates in all levels of campaigns, from presidential elections to local mayoral elections, run an effective campaign. Candidates who sought my help include the current president of Korea Muhyun No, the current Mayor of Seoul MyungBak Lee, a few governors, many parliamentary members, as well as mayors of local cities. I also gave a number of lectures on campaign strategies for candidates in the election committee of the central government, and in special programs organized by universities, news organizations, and social associations.

In the process of accumulating knowledge of campaign strategies, I worked as a director of one of the leading survey companies, Research and Research Inc., and founded Camst Inc., a consulting company for helping candidates with their campaign strategies in Korea. In addition to my consulting work, I wrote and published five books in Korean about campaign strategies, entitled *Campaign Strategies* (1996), *Elections and Polls* (1997), *Modern Society and Public Opinion* (2000), *Theories and Practices of Political Campaign Strategies* (2000), and *Winning Strategies* (2002). I also created three computer software, *A Program for Strategies, A Program for Selecting Targets*, and *A Database*, in which I offer particular programs to help a candidate calculate and plan the steps he or she needs to take in order to run a successful campaign. Almost all of the candidates who consulted my services and who used the computer software that I created in fact won the office for which they were running.

The principles of campaign strategies discussed in this book can be applied to any election in any democratic country, just as war strategies or marketing strategies can be applied universally. The only real differences among elections are procedural details and the rules of an election, and any problems that come up as a result of these differences can be easily solved when one has the essential knowledge of campaign strategies. Therefore, a candidate who acquires important tips and information about campaign strategies through this book and who applies them to his/her campaign certainly has a high probability of winning an election.

Most examples of Korea in this book come from my first-hand experience, as is most survey data used in this book obtained from surveys conducted under my supervision. In some cases, where the data was confidential, the names are initialized.

While this book is primarily for candidates and their staff members, it is also useful for campaign consultants and college students, as it includes new methodologies of campaign strategies. In fact, the Korean version of this book has been used by political consultants and pollsters as a guide and also was unexpectedly selected as a core textbook in many universities in Korea. It is my hope that readers will benefit from this book and will win whatever election in which they are running.

Acknowledgments

I thank my clients and the employees of Camst Company who have been an inspiration to me while I researched and wrote this book. I also thank Professor Paul Beck, Chairman of the Department of Political Science at The Ohio State University, who invited me to the department as a visiting scholar. Without his invitation, I could not have completed this book. I also greatly thank Professor Anthony Mughan who helped me as a dissertation advisor. He has published numerous valuable articles and books. His work has inspired me in turn to work, research, and publish.

My thanks also go to Professor Daniel Shea of the Department of Political Science of Allegheny College who reviewed and commented on this book. I think his *Campaign Craft* is the best book in the field of campaign strategy I have ever read. I also want to thank Dr. Müge Galin, English instructor at The Ohio State University and editor, who reviewed and corrected every sentence in this book.

My wife Kyung, daughter Hyein, and son Jay always encourage me to do what I want. I deeply appreciate their lifelong support and love. Without my mother, I could not have come to where I am today. She raised me by herself since my father died when I was five years old, and she has supported me mentally and financially. I am deeply grateful to her. Finally, I must send my greatest thanks to God who always takes care of my family.

Chapter 1
Introduction

Candidates run to win. How glorious it is to win in an election! In the meantime, how painful is losing! The famous British Conservative politician Winston Churchill once expressed such a feeling, thus: "[losing an election] is like a sea-beast fished up from the depths, a diver too suddenly hoisted, my veins threatened to burst from the fall in pressure."[1] Then how does one make sure to win in an election?

Victory in most elections comes with good campaign strategies. Most elections that are carried out in democratic countries are not decided by all voters in a district, but by the support of some voters, whose choice has been completely directed by candidates' campaign strategies. Consequently, campaign strategies to get support from those core voters greatly influence the results of an election, especially in elections where there are a large number of undecided voters and the difference of support between the candidates is less than 10%. Therefore, a candidate who does not have a clear strategy for running his or her campaign is rather handicapped and does not have a high probability of winning.

Only politicians who win with good campaign strategies and who have

---

[1] Henry Pelling, *Winston Churchill* (London: Macmillan, 1974) 563.

cultivated a strategic mind can solve the various complex problems that they encounter in office satisfactorily once they get elected. Therefore, it is strongly recommended that all candidates must acquire knowledge of campaign strategies before diving into a campaign.

It is also recommended that candidates plan their campaign strategies before they begin campaigning, because it is very difficult to implement campaign strategies devised while campaigning. Usually, candidates who have completed their campaign plans before the campaign begins are likely to win an election. Winners, such as Ronald Reagan in 1984, George Bush in 1988 and Bill Clinton in 1992 and 1996, had completed their campaign strategies before the convention for nomination. In contrast, Hurbert Humhprey in 1968, Michael Dukakis in 1988, and George Bush in 1992, who lost the presidential elections in which they ran, had devised their strategies after their nominations.[2]

1. What Kind of Game is an Election?

An election has three characteristics.

(1) An Election is a Game in which All Candidates must Reveal their Strategies and Tactics to their Opponents

Since an election is the process in which a candidate persuades voters to support him/her in public, candidates cannot conceal their strategies and tactics from their opponents. In fact, a professional political campaign strategist can abstractly know a candidate's strategies by listening to his/her campaign address just once.

---

[2] Stephen Wayne, *The Road to the White House 2000:The Politics of Presidential Election* (New York: Bedford/St. Martin's, 2000) 198-99.

(2) An Election is an Unfair Game

It may not be true that every candidate's campaign is conducted under the same conditions. For example, in high-profile races such as the presidential election, the mass media pays more attention to candidates nominated by one of the main political parties and those who are highly probable to be elected. In the meantime, other minor candidates campaign without free media. It may not be also true that every candidate campaigns under fair rules. For instance, Korea's electoral law permits parliamentary members to hold an unlimited number of meetings to report their performance to their constituents anytime, while it prohibits challengers to hold such meetings, except for the official campaign period of 16 days.

(3) An Election is a Game in which Mistakes are Made in Strategies and Tactics too Frequently

Candidates and their staff members usually do not make a great effort to understand and analyze the characteristics of voters scientifically. As a result, almost all candidates campaign with wrong strategies and tactics due to abstract information about voters' characteristics.

2. Two Dimensions of Campaign Strategies

Concepts related to winning in an election are called "campaign strategies." Campaign strategies, thus, are defined by the planned behavior of candidates to win or to get more votes by effectively using their personnel and material resources.[3] Campaign strategies can be divided into two dimensions: checking the probability of winning before deciding to run and establishing a strategy after deciding to run.

---

[3] The League of Woman Voters of California Education Fund, *Choosing the President* (New York: Lyons & Burford, 1992) 80; Fank Soruaf and Paul Beck, *Party Politics in America* (Boston: Scott, Foresman and Company, 1988) 288.

(1) First Dimension: Checking the Probability of Winning

The results of some elections in democratic countries are already determined well before candidates decide to run. Therefore, candidates must check the probability of winning through vulnerability/feasibility surveys when they are considering to run for office. A candidate must run only when his/her probability of getting elected is high.

For example, in parliamentary elections in Korea, a candidate nominated by a major party receives around 20% of the total votes based on voters' party preference, while it is very rare to find a candidate who can gain more than 15% of the total votes based on his/her personal image and career. This means that it is very difficult for candidates from minor parties and independent candidates to win in an election in Korea. Therefore, candidates from minor parties and independent candidates would be encouraged to give up their candidacy. This phenomenon can be easily seen in all democratic countries.

(2) Second Dimension: Establishing a Strategy after Deciding to Run

This book is mainly about the second dimension of a campaign strategy that is about how well candidates set up their strategies after they decide to run. In this stage, candidates and their staff members must accurately predict what happens in the process of a campaign and determine what they will do in order to effectively get votes based on the predictions. In the United States, where candidates campaign for the primaries before an election, knowledge of the second dimension is also extremely useful during the primaries.

This book will elaborate on the following points necessary for running an effective campaign.

①Methods to predict variations of candidate support, which is critically important for effective planning and implementation of campaign strategies

② Five concepts of campaign strategies

③ Methods to establish various targets, such as (a) *target for raising recognition,* (b) *target voters,* (c) *target opponent* and (d) *target for increasing supporters' voting rate*

④ Concepts of a candidate's image and how to create a desirable image

⑤ Methods to plan strategies related to themes and policies

⑥ Analysis of the characteristics of a campaign organization and how to build an effective organization

⑦ Kinds of campaigns and checking their effectiveness

⑧ Methods to effectively distribute resources

⑨ Private surveys used for campaign strategies

⑩ Methods to analyze and interpret private surveys

⑪ Four requirements for a successful campaign strategist

Chapter 2
Prediction of Variations in Support for a Candidate

1. Factors Influencing Support for a Candidate

Candidates and their staff must roughly predict variations in support, in order to establish a proper direction of their strategies and select appropriate campaign activities. Variations in support for a candidate depend mainly on the length of the duration of campaign activities, the amount of information delivered to voters about the election, the number of the main candidates, and the degree of voters' recognition of candidates early in the campaign.

(1) The Length of the Duration of Campaign Activities

Variations in support for a candidate are closely related to the length of the duration of campaign activities. The longer the duration of campaign activities, the greater the variations in support for a candidate.

The duration of a campaign refers to the term during which candidates actually carry out campaign activities rather than the term stipulated by the election law. For example, candidates in Korea usually engage in campaign activities for a longer time than the duration stipulated by the law. In detail, the official duration of a campaign for candidates for Korea's parliamentary election is only 16 days. However, most candidates begin to campaign far before the official starting date of a campaign. Some even start 2-3 years before Election Day.

(2) The Amount of Information Delivered to Voters

The more information about the election that is delivered to voters, the greater the variations in support for a candidate. The amount of information delivered to voters is usually decided by three factors. The first is the degree to which voters are interest in the election. When voters are highly interested in an election, variations in support for a candidate are also wide, because there is a great deal of transfer of information about the election to voters.

The second factor that influences the amount of information delivered to voters is how closely the mass media pays attention to the election. In an election in which the mass media illuminates the election with great interest, there is naturally quite a bit of information about the election transmitted to voters. Such vast information results in wide variations in support for a candidate. Voters usually are interested in (a) the presidential election, (b) congressional- and governor's election, and (c) the mayoral election, in that order. This is because the mass media pays attention to these elections in that order. Therefore, the degree of variations in support for a candidate also generally follows the same order.

The third factor that influences the amount of information delivered to voters is the degree of homogeneity among voters in the district. Homogeneous voters are more apt to transfer information among themselves than heterogeneous voters; consequently, the more homogeneous the voters, the more the variations in support among them.

(3) Voters' Recognition of Candidates Early in a Campaign

In a district where voters highly recognize candidates early in a campaign, most voters tend to decide early whom they will support, and the number of undecided voters is not so great. As a result, wide variations in support for a candidate are hardly expected in this district during the campaign period. In contrast, in a district where voters do not recognize all of the candidates very well, variations in support for a candidate are likely to be wide during the campaign period, because rapid increase in voters' recognition of candidates is connected with variations in support.

(4) The Number of Main Candidates

Main candidates are those who are likely to win. They are usually candidates nominated by major political parties or popular independent candidates. The greater the number of main candidates, the less variations there are in candidate support, since the main candidates already have many fixed supporters. Therefore, when the number of the main candidates increases, the number of undecided voters decreases. The fewer the number of undecided voters, the less variations there are in candidate support during the campaign period.

2. Elections of Minimum and Maximum Variations in Support for a Candidate

As seen in Figure 2.1, minimum variations in support for a candidate are expected in an election in which the following conditions are met: the duration of the campaign period is short, the amount of information about the election delivered to voters is not much, voters recognize all candidates well early in the campaign, and there are a large number of main candidates. In contrast, maximum variations in support for a candidate are predicted in an election in which the duration of a campaign is long, there is a lot of information delivered to voters, voters do not recognize all candidates very well, and there are only two main candidates.

Figure 2.1 Elections of maximum and minimum variations in support

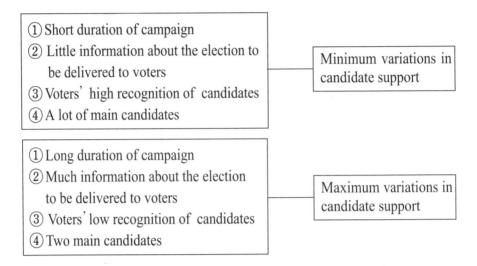

3. Proper Campaign Strategies under Different Circumstances

Campaign strategists must plan the direction of their strategy depending on the duration of the campaign period and the amount of information about the election to be delivered to voters.

(1) When the Duration of a Campaign is Long and there is much Information to be Delivered to Voters

① Prepare Proper Responses to a Negative Campaign by Opponents

A candidate's weaknesses brought up by opponents are easily disseminated through the mass media and/or by word of mouth. Therefore, candidates must prepare appropriate responses to negative campaigning against themselves.

② Be Consistent in Issue Positions or Political Views

A candidate's inconsistent issue positions or political views can easily become a problem, particularly in presidential and governor's elections, where the mass media are paying close attention. For example, in the 1984

U.S. presidential election, in an effort to point out contradictory actions and comments of the Democratic candidate Walter Mondale, the Republicans produced a 200-page record of his speeches, promises, and claims.[4] Therefore, it is essential that candidates stick to the same political views from the start of the campaign to the end.

③ Do not Focus too much on Negative Campaigning against Opponents

Voters get tired of a candidate who only repeats negative campaign slogans against his/her opponents and does very little positive campaigning for him/herself. Therefore, a candidate must properly combine positive campaigning for him/herself and negative campaigning against his/her opponents.

(2) When the Duration of a Campaign is Short and there is not much Information to be Delivered to Voters

① Utilize Public Opinion Leaders

Since a candidate cannot get in touch with many voters face-to-face, he/she must utilize public opinion leaders in the district who can deliver a good impression of him/her to voters.

② The Number of Issues must be Curtailed

Voters cannot get interested in and be bombarded with too many issues. Therefore, candidates should campaign with very few issues with which voters would be most concerned.

4. Prediction of Variations in Support for a Candidate based on a Survey of Public Opinion

A survey of public opinion can allow campaign strategists to make predictions in the variations in support for a candidate. It helps them to look

---

[4] Daniel Shea, *Campaign Craft* (London: Praeger, 1996) 71.

at the increase of voters' recognition of candidates or to compare present and past voting patterns to make their predictions.

(1) Predicting the Variations in Support for a Candidate based on the Increase of Voters' Recognition of Candidates

Support for a candidate normally increases, when voters' recognition of him/her increases, since many undecided voters will determine the candidate they support after they have information about a candidate's image, career, and attainments in scholarship and so on.

Figure 2.2 Change in candidate support according to change in voters' recognition of candidates

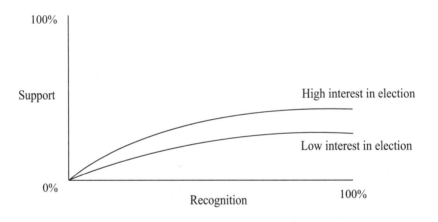

However, the increase in candidate support is always less than the increase in voters' recognition of candidates. The reason is that some voters who newly recognize the candidate decide to support him/her because they are satisfied with his/her ability and so on, others do not, because they are disappointed with him/her in certain respects.

As Figure 2.2 shows, the increasing gap of a candidate's support is reduced when voters' recognition of a candidate is closer to 100%. For example, if support for a certain candidate increases only by 4% when voters' recognition of him/her increases by 10% from 50% to 60%, support for that candidate normally increases by less than 4% when voters' recognition of him/her increases by 10% from 80% to 90%. This occurs because voters recognizing candidates later than others are not usually interested in the election; therefore, they have a higher probability not to decide on a candidate to support even after they have gotten to know all of the candidates. By the same principle, as Figure2.2 shows, the rising gap of candidate support caused by increase in voters' recognition of candidates is greater in a high-profile election than in a low-profile election, because voters are more interested in the high-profile election.

(a) Method to Predict how much the Increase in Voters' Recognition of Candidates Impacts the Increase in Candidate Support

Candidate support increases greatly with the rise of voters' recognition of candidates in a district where almost none of the voters recognize all of the candidates. However, support for a candidate increases moderately in a district where voters already recognize all of the candidates very well.

In a district where voters (hereafter called *split-ticket voters*) support a candidate because they like that candidate's career and image regardless of the candidate's party affiliation, we can see a high increase in candidate support caused by an increase in voters' recognition of the candidates. Meanwhile, in a district where voters (hereafter called *straight-ticket voters*) support a candidate because they are committed to that candidate's party, the increase in voters' recognition of the candidates results in only a small increase in candidate support.

Table 2.1 shows variations in support when two factors described above are considered simultaneously. In a district where the number of *straight-ticket voters* is great and voters' recognition of candidates early in a campaign is already high, it is hardly expected that candidate support would rapidly increase due to an increase in voters' recognition of candidates during the campaign period.

Candidate support somewhat increases due to an increase in voters' recognition of candidates in a district where voters' recognition of candidates early in the campaign is high, but the number of *straight-ticket voters* is small, as is true in a district where voters' recognition of candidates early in a campaign is low, but the number of *straight-ticket voters* is large.

In the meantime, candidate support considerably increases according to an increase in voters' recognition of candidates in a district where voters' recognition of candidates early in the campaign is low and the number of *straight-ticket voters* is small.

Table 2.1 Variations in candidate support due to the increase in voters' recognition of candidates

| | | Voters' recognition of candidates | |
		High	Low
Number of straight-ticket voters	Great	Low	Middle
	Small	Middle	High

(b) Examples of Predicting Variations in Support for a Candidate based on Private Surveys

Variations in support for a candidate can be predicted based either on a one-time private survey or multiple private surveys.

(b.1) Hypothetical Examples of Prediction based on a One-Time Private Survey[5]

Following are examples in which a certain candidate is likely to win and an example in which a close election is anticipated.

---

[5] The private survey means a survey conducted for a certain candidate.

Case in which Candidate X is likely to win

X and Y are candidates nominated by main political parties. Based on the results of a private survey conducted on the 60th day before Election Day, Table 2.2 indicates that *straight-ticket voters* make up 30% of the total voters and each candidate shares 15% of the *straight-ticket voters*. *Split-ticket voters* who support Candidate X make up 20% of the total voters, and voters who recognize Candidate X make up 60% of the total voters. This means that around one third of the voters who recognize Candidate X consists of *split-ticket voters* supporting Candidate X.

Split-ticket voters supporting Candidate Y make up 10% of the total voters and voters who recognize Candidate Y make up 40% of the total voters. This means that about one fourth of the voters who recognize Candidate Y consist of *split-ticket voters* who support Candidate Y.

The following prediction can be made based on the results of the private survey. If voters' recognition of Candidate Y reaches 60% from the current 40%, it is likely that the number of *split-ticket voters* who support Candidate Y may go up by about 5%. Thus, support for Candidate Y becomes 15%, which is 5% less than support for Candidate X when voters' recognition of Candidate X is still 60% of the total voters. Then, the probability that Candidate X wins over Candidate Y is a little greater than that of the reverse case.

Table 2.2 Results of a private survey conducted on the 60th day before Election Day

Candidate	Voters' recognition of candidate	Support of split-ticket voters	Undecided voters	Support of straight-ticket voters	Ratio of voters' recognition of candidate to support of split-ticket voters
X	60%	20%	40%	15%	3 : 1
Y	40%	10%		15%	4 : 1

Case in which a Close Election is Anticipated

X and Y are candidates nominated by main political parties. Based on the results of a private survey conducted on the 60th day before Election Day, Table 2.3 indicates that *straight-ticket voters* make up 30% of the total voters and each candidate shares 15% of the *straight-ticket voters*.

Out of the total voters, 50% recognizes Candidate X and 25% represents the *split-ticket voters* who support Candidate X. This means that half of the voters who recognize Candidate X are *split-ticket voters* who support him/her.

Voters who recognize Candidate Y make up 40% of the total voters and *split-ticket voters* who support Candidate Y make up 20% of the total voters. This means that about half of the voters who recognize Candidate Y are *split-ticket voters* who support him/her.

The following prediction can be made based on the results of the private survey. If voters' recognition of Candidate Y reaches 60% from the current 40%, it is likely that *split-ticket voters* supporting Candidate Y may go up by about 10%. In other words, when voters' recognition of both candidates is the same at 60%, support for Candidate X is similar to that for Candidate Y. Then, it is very difficult to predict which candidate might win.

Table 2.3 Results of a private survey conducted on the 60th day before Election Day

Candidate	Voters' recognition of candidate	Support of split-ticket voters	Undecided voters	Support of straight-ticket voters	Ratio of voters' recognition of candidate to support of split-ticket voters
X	50%	25%	25%	15%	2 : 1
Y	40%	20%		15%	2 : 1

Case in which Candidate Y Wins

X and Y are candidates nominated by main political parties. Table 2.4 indicates based on the results of a private survey conducted on the 60th day before Election Day that *straight-ticket voters* make up 30% of the total voters, and each candidate shares 15% of the *straight-ticket voters*. Voters who recognize Candidate X make up 90% of the total voters and *split-ticket voters* who support Candidate X make up 10% of the total voters. This means that one ninth of the voters who recognize Candidate X consists of *split-ticket voters* who support Candidate X.

Split-ticket voters who support Candidate Y make up 10% of the total voters and voters who recognize Candidate Y make up 30% of the total voters. This means that one third of the voters who recognize Candidate Y consists of *split-ticket voters* who support Candidate Y.

The following prediction can be made based on the results of the private survey. Since voters' recognition of Candidate X is already 90%, it is very difficult to raise this number any further. This means that Candidate X has difficulty in raising support for him/herself.

On the other hand, because voters who recognize Candidate Y make up only 30% of the total voters, their numbers can increase to about 80% of the total voters. When voters who recognize Candidate Y make up 80% of the

Table 2.4 Results of a private survey conducted on the 60th day before Election Day

Candidate	Voters' recognition of candidate	Support of split-ticket voters	Undecided voters	Support of straight-ticket voters	Ratio of voters' recognition of candidate to support of split-ticket voters
X	90%	10%	50%	15%	9 : 1
Y	30%	10%		15%	3 : 1

total voters, the number of the *split-ticket voters* who support him/her will go up by at least 15%. Thus, support for Candidate Y will be more than 25%, which is 15% more than support for Candidate X. This means that Candidate Y will probably win over Candidate X in the end.

(b.2) Real Example of Predicting Variations in Support for a Candidate based on a One-Time Private Survey

Candidate Dae C. Jung, seen in Table 2.5, was an incumbent running for a parliamentary election in 1996 in a district in Seoul. He and his family were very popular in the district, because he had been elected four times in this district and his father had been elected several times in the same district.

Meanwhile, Candidate Sung B. Park, the main opponent of Candidate Jung, had been a news anchor of a major broadcasting company but was a newcomer to the district.

A private survey conducted 45 days before Election Day showed that 91.2% of the total voters recognized Candidate Jung and only 66.9% of the total voters recognized Candidate Park. Candidate Jung led Candidate Park by 11.5% in candidate support, while 45.6% of the total voters was undecided.

The election turned out to be the defeat of Candidate Jung by 9.8%. As the

Table 2.5 Results of a private survey conducted on the 45th day before Election Day & results of the election

		Candidate Dae C. Jung	Candidate Sung B. Park	Undecided voters
45th day before Election Day	Voters' recognition of candidate	91.2%	66.9%	45.6%
	Voters' support for candidate	26.5%	15.0%	
Results of the election		42.0%	51.8%	-

campaign proceeded and more voters recognized Candidate Park and support for him increased. Meanwhile, support for Candidate Jung remained the same, because he was already fully recognized by voters early in the campaign. This means that most of the undecided voters (45.6% of total voters) eventually voted for Candidate Park.

(b.3) Hypothetical Example of Prediction based on Two Private Surveys

One private survey is not enough to make an accurate prediction, because it is very difficult to tell accurately from only one survey the degree of change in support caused by the degree of shift in voters' recognition of candidates. Therefore, to make an accurate prediction, the results of at least two private surveys must be compared.

Table 2.6 shows the results of two private surveys conducted 20 and 30 days before an election for which two candidates run. *Straight-ticket voters* make up 30% of the total voters and each candidate has 15% of the *straight-ticket voters*.

When voters' recognition of Candidate X increases from 70% to 80%, support for him/her may increase by 2%. When voters' recognition of Candidate Y increases from 50% to 70%, support for him/her may go up by 4%. That is, the two candidates' chances are the same, in that when voters' recognition of them rises by 10%, support for them goes up by 2%.

Then it can be predicted that Candidate X is likely to win over Candidate Y, because when voters' recognition of both candidates reaches 90%, support for Candidate X is around 44% and support for Candidate Y is around 38%.

(2) Predicting the Variations in Support for a Candidate based on Comparing Present and Past Voting Patterns in a Private Survey

(a) Prediction based on Changes in Supporters of Two Same Kinds of Recent Elections in a Private Survey

Table 2.7 indicates the results of a hypothetical private survey conducted

Table 2.6 Results of private surveys conducted on the 30th day and the 20th day before Election Day for measuring voters' recognition of, and support for candidates

		Candidate X	Candidate Y
30th day before Election Day	Voters' recognition of candidate	70%	50%
	Voters' support for candidate	40%	30%
	Undecided voters	30%	
20th day before Election Day	Voters' recognition of candidate	80%	70%
	Voters' support for candidate	42%	34%
	Undecided voters	24%	
Change in voters' recognition		+10%	+20%
Change in support		+2%	+4%
Change in candidate support caused by a 10% change in voters' recognition		+2%	+2%
Expected support for a candidate when voters' recognition of the candidate reaches 90%		44%	38%
Straight-ticket voters		15%	15%

for a district in which the same candidates run for two consecutive elections, the forthcoming election and the past election. Sixty days before Election Day, support for both candidates is the same at 30%, and for undecided voters, it is 40%.

Table 2.7 Results of a private survey conducted on the 60th day before Election Day

	Candidate X	Candidate Y	Undecided voters
Support	30%	30%	40%

Table 2.8 Results of a cross-analysis of the responses to questions, "*For whom did you cast a vote in the last election?*" and "*Whom will you support in the upcoming election?*"

		Support on the 60th day before Election Day		
		Candidate X	Candidate Y	Undecided voters
Support in the last election	Candidate X	40%	20%	40%
	Candidate Y	5%	85%	10%

As shown in Table 2.8, the answers of only 40% of the total voters casting votes for Candidate X in the last election indicate that they would vote for him/her in this election, while 20% would cast votes for Candidate Y, and 40% is undecided. Out of the voters casting votes for Candidate Y in the last election, the answers of 85% indicate that they would vote for him/her again, while 5% would cast votes for Candidate X, and 10% is undecided. Candidates such as X are usually ones who were not as active when they were in office as their constituents expected them to be. It means that when the campaign proceeds, support for Candidate X is likely to rise slowly, while support for Candidate Y may go up rapidly.

(b) Prediction based on Changes in Supporters of Two Different Kinds of Recent Elections in a Private Survey

<u>Hypothetical Example</u>

Table 2.9 shows the results of a private survey conducted for a parliamentary district, in which there exists a strong regionalism leaning toward Party X. Support for Candidate C of Party X is 35%; support for Candidate D of Party Y is 40%; and for the undecided voters, it is 25%.

Table 2.9 Results of a private survey conducted on the 60th day before Election Day

	Candidate C of Party X	Candidate D of Party Y	Undecided voters
Support	35%	40%	25%

Table 2.10 shows a cross-analysis of responses to two questions, *"Whom did you support in the governor's election one year ago?"* and *"Whom will you support in the forthcoming parliamentary election?"* Of the voters who supported Candidate A of Party X in the last election, the answers of 40% indicate that they would support Candidate C of Party X in the upcoming election, while 10% would support Candidate D of Party Y, and 50% is undecided.

On the other hand, the answers of 80% of the voters who supported Candidate B of Party Y in the last election indicate that they would support Candidate D of Party Y in the forthcoming election, while 5% would support Candidate C of Party X, and 15% is undecided.

Table 2.10 Results of a cross-analysis of responses to questions, *"Whom did you support in the governor's election one year ago?"* and *"Whom will you support in the forthcoming parliamentary election?"*

		Support on the 60th day before Election Day in the forthcoming election		
		Candidate C of Party X	Candidate D of Party Y	Undecided voters
Support in the last governor's election	Candidate A of Party X	40%	10%	50%
	Candidate B of Party Y	5%	80%	15%

Based on the cross-analysis above, we can predict that Candidate C may win over Candidate D, although Candidate C is now 5% behind Candidate D in candidate support. Exactly 50% of voters who voted for Party X in the last governor's election remains undecided. However, they are highly likely to vote for Candidate C of Party X because of regionalism leaning toward Party X. This means that it is anticipated that approaching Election Day, support for Candidate C of Party X may rise rapidly.

Meanwhile, 15% of voters who voted for Party Y in the last governor's election remains undecided. Most of them may not vote for Candidate D of Party Y, because regionalism in this district is not in favor of him/her. Then, support for Candidate D may rarely increase; consequently, he/she may be outpaced by Candidate C in the end.

Real Example

The following example is based on a private survey conducted on the 26th day before Election Day of the 1998 governor's election of Kyungki Province in Korea. Table 2.11 shows a cross-analysis of responses to two questions, *"For whom did you cast a vote in the last presidential election?"* and *"Whom will you support in the forthcoming governor's election in Kyungki Province?"* Out of the voters who supported Candidate Hoichang Lee of Party Hannara in the 1997 presidential election in Korea,[6] 51.2% responded that they would support Candidate Hakkyu Sohn of Party Hannara in the forthcoming governor's election; 50.3% of the voters who supported Daejung Kim of Party Kookmin Council in the last presidential election responded that they would support Candidate Changyeol Lim of Party Kookmin Council in the governor's election. Thus, the two parties were not much different in the number of supporters who continued to support the same party in the two elections.

---

[6] Candidate Daejung Kim of Party Kookmin Council won over Candidate Hoichang Lee of Party Hannara by 1.3% in this presidential election.

Table 2.11 Cross-analysis of responses to questions, *"For whom did you cast a vote in the last presidential election?"* **and** *"Whom will you support in the forthcoming governor's election in Kyungki Province?"*

		Support in the forthcoming governor's election in Kyungki Province		
		Hakkyu Sohn of Party Hannara	Changyeol Lim of Party Kookmin Council	Undecided voters
Support in the last presidential election	Hoichang Lee of Party Hannara	51.2%	17.3%	31.5%
	Daejung Kim of Party Kookmin Council	12.1%	50.3%	37.6%
	Injae Lee of Party Kookminshindang	24.6%	22.5%	52.9%

Table 2.12 Comparison of results of the private survey conducted on the 26th day before Election Day with results of the election.

	Candidate Hakkyu Sohn of Party Hannara	Candidate Changyeol Lim of Party Kookmin Council	Undecided voters
Results of a private survey	21.5%	34.3%	44.2%
Results of the election	45.7%	54.3%	

However, Candidate Lim of Party Kookmin Council was in a little more favorable position than Candidate Sohn of Party Hannara in swing voters, who switch from party to party in different elections. Of the voters who supported Hoichang Lee of Party Hannara in the presidential election, 17.3% responded that they would support Candidate Lim of Party Kookmin Council in the upcoming governor's election. Of the voters who supported Candidate Daejung Kim of Party Kookmin Council in the presidential election, 12.1% responded that they would support Candidate Sohn of Party Hannara.

In the meantime, the number of undecided voters was a little higher in support for Daejung Kim of Party Kookmin Council than the number of supporters for Hoichang Lee of Party Hannara. Among the voters who supported the third candidate, Injae Lee of Party Kookminshindang in the 1997 presidential election, 24.6% responded that they would support Candidate Sohn of Party Hannara in the upcoming governor's election; 22.5% responded that they would support Candidate Lim of Party Kookmin Council. A cross-analysis based on this survey can predict that Candiate Lim of Party Kookmin Council would be in a little more favorable position on Election Day than Candidate Sohn of Party Hannara.

The election results were in fact not so different from this prediction. As seen in Table 2.12, the private survey that was conducted 26 days before Election Day showed that Candidate Lim of Party Kookmin Council led Candidate Sohn of Party Hannara by 12.8% in candidate support and in fact won the election by an 8.6% margin.

Chapter 3
Five Concepts of Campaign Strategies

Campaign strategies are based on a simple but important principle: to inform voters about only his/her strong points, pointing out only his/her opponents' shortcomings. On the basis of this principle, five concepts of campaign strategies are developed. These are *strategies to make up for a candidate's shortcomings, negative strategies, positive strategies, comparative strategies, and responsive strategies.*[7]

1. *Strategies to Make up for a Candidate's Shortcomings*
Candidates use these strategies to make up for their shortcomings in advance, in order to prevent negative campaigning about them by their opponents. Such a strategy must be completed before a campaign begins. For example, a candidate whose weak point is unfair wealth accumulation can avoid attack against him/herself by establishing a scholarship foundation or financially supporting citizens who have had a misfortune.

Such strategies are usually more crucial for rookie candidates than for

---

[7] The concepts of four strategies, except for *strategies to make up for a candidate's shortcomings,* are in accord with "negative messages", "positive messages", "comparative messages", and "responsive messages" each in *Candidates, Parties, and Campaigns* by Barbara Salmore and Stephen Salmore (Washington, D.C.: Congressional Quarterly, Inc., 1989) 147-148.

career candidates. Since the weak points of career candidates, who have run for elections several times, may be already revealed and reflected in the candidate support they receive, *strategies to make up for a candidate's shortcomings* may not be very crucial to career candidates. In contrast, a rookie candidate's critical weak points revealed by his/her opponents could be fatal to him/her, because voters expect the record of a rookie candidate to be clean in every respect.

In the case of the Democratic Party in the United States, the party's weak point was that immediately following the Clinton scandal with Monica Lewinsky, the party was viewed especially as too "liberal," which hurt Candidate Al Gore's campaign for the 2000 presidency and became a weakness when he ran against Candidate George W. Bush. Candidate Gore's strategy to overcome this weakness was to distance himself from President Clinton and to avoid too much publicity in association with President Clinton, for fear that the public would equate the two men and regard Candidate Gore as being too liberal. Candidate Gore also made sure to have a lot of photo opportunities that included his wife and children. However, these efforts were not enough for him to win the election

In general, all kinds of shortcomings can be made up with an appropriate strategy that is intentionally targeted to cover up a candidate's particular shortcoming. For example, President Ronald Reagan who ran for his second term at the age of 73 was accused of being too old and forgetful as compared with his opponent, Walter Mondale, who was 56 years old at the time.

However, his campaign managers used a strategy of arguing that he was experienced and wise, and it worked. In the debates, President Reagan in fact successfully accused Candidate Mondale of being too young and inexperienced. Consequently, President Reagan was elected for a second term by a landslide.

However, some weaknesses cannot be covered up. For example, a candidate who has a serious criminal record cannot completely make up for it, because he/she cannot remove it permanently from his/her record.

2. *Negative Strategies*

These strategies, well known as the *negative campaign,* involve criticizing the opponent's weak points. They are used for a candidate to persuade his/her opponents' supporters and undecided voters not to vote for the opponent.

(1) Reasons to Use *Negative Strategies*

There are two reasons why candidates use negative strategies. First, voters momentarily tend to hate candidates' criticism of their opponents. However, when voters hear the criticism over again, they tend to begin to believe it and not to vote for the criticized candidate. Second, voters tend to pay more attention to criticism than applause on candidates. Then, in elections in which the campaign period is not long and available funds for each candidate are very confined, it is more effective for a candidate to criticize his/her opponent's weak points in order to lower support for his/her opponent, rather than inform voters of his/her own strong points in order to raise support for him/herself.

(2) Results of Successful *Negative Strategies*

If there are only two candidates, and only one of them is successful in criticizing the other, some of the voters who turn their backs on the criticized candidate will support the candidate who is doing the criticism. However, if there are more than three candidates, voters who turn their backs on the criticized candidate do not guarantee to support the candidate who is doing the criticizing. If support for all three candidates is about the same and a candidate predicts that voters who turn their backs on the criticized candidate will support the third candidate, then he/she should not engage in negative campaigning. Therefore, candidates must anticipate which candidate the betrayed voters of the criticized candidate would support, before they go ahead with their negative campaigning.

(3) Four Suggestions for *Negative Strategies*

① It is usually not desirable to use *negative strategies* too early in a campaign, for the following two reasons. First, it is easy for voters to forget the content of negative strategies on Election Day. Second, negative strategies early in a campaign provide the criticized candidate with sufficient time to recover from the criticism.

② It is good to repeat the criticism of the opponents as frequently as possible, because success of *negative strategies* depends on how frequently the same criticism is repeated. At first, voters are half in doubt about the criticism. However, when the criticism is repeated, voters begin to believe it.

③ It may not be a good idea to criticize a candidate's being unknown to voters. *Negative strategies* against poorly recognized opponents only increase the voters' recognition of them, rather than decreasing voters' support for them.

④ Candidates who are at a disadvantage when voters' voting rate is lower are better not to do too much criticism. Voters' sneer at an election caused by too much criticism keeps some of the voters from going to the polls at all.

(4) Four Ways to Cope with an Opponent's *Negative Strategies*

① Counterattacking the Opponent by Criticizing his/her Weakness

This is used only when voters have more interest in a candidate's criticism of the opponent's weakness than vice versa. When this is successful, the candidate can escape the opponent's negative campaign against him/herself, since it is difficult for the opponent to continue negative campaigning against the candidate when he/she must first respond to criticism of him/herself.

② Counteracting Criticism by Offering Clear Evidence

This is used only when the content of criticism of a candidate is false. When this strategy is successful, the opponent doing the criticism becomes an untrustworthy person and can even be sued for malicious propaganda. However, although a candidate has clear evidence to counteract the opponent's criticism of him/herself, the candidate must not do so, if he/she does not have enough time before Election Day to provide such evidence to voters.

③ Confirming Content of Criticism to Prevent it from being Greatly Diffused

It is better for a candidate to admit that criticism of him/her is true as soon as possible, when the criticism is likely to turn out to be true in the end, and when the mass media is apt to pay continuous attention to it until it turns out to be true. Delay of admission only allows the criticism to spread to voters more. However, this is definitely a method that candidates prefer to avoid.

④ Not Responding to Criticism

There are two instances in which a candidate can ignore criticism of him/herself. The first is when the criticism does not have a significant influence on the final consequence of an election. The second is when the candidate's response to the criticism only raises voters' recognition of his/her opponents by arousing voters' interest in the election.

3. Positive Strategies[8]

These strategies are used to raise support for a candidate by notifying his/her strong point to voters. They are usually used under the following circumstances.

---

[8] This method is also named "Stand Alone" in Campaigns & Elections, *The Road to Victory* (Dubuque, Iowa, 1995) 4.

① A candidate's opponents do not have any crucial weak points. Then, the candidate cannot use a *negative campaign* against his/her opponents.
② A candidate's opponents are not in competition with the candidate, so that he/she can win without using a *negative campaign* against his/her opponents.

Generally, *positive strategies* are regarded as the most ineffective, because voters are least interest in the candidate who only tries to point out his/her strong points to them.

4. *Comparative Strategies*[9]

These strategies are a combination of *negative-* and *positive strategies*. In detail, they are used to increase support for a candidate by pointing out his/her strong points to voters, while criticizing his/her opponents' weak points in order to voters not to vote for the opponents. These strategies are most frequently used by a candidate challenging an incumbent.

For example, the British Conservative Party in opposition used *comparative strategies* as seen in its following platform in the 1970 parliamentary election.

"Now our country suffers from the worst inflation caused by taxes raised by the Labor Party. The Conservative Party will solve this problem by cutting taxes, reducing government expenses and increasing savings."[10]

Figure 3.1 shows an analysis of the British Conservative Party's platform.

Comparative strategies were also used in the 1997 presidential election in Korea, in which three candidates ran: Candidate Hoichang Lee of Party

---

[9]　This method is also named *"Mirror Opposite,"* in Campaigns & Elections, *The Road to Victory, 4.*
[10]　The Conservative Party, *A Better Tomorrow* (London: The Conservative Party, 1970).

Figure 3.1 *Comparative strategies* **of the British Conservative Party in the 1970 Election.**

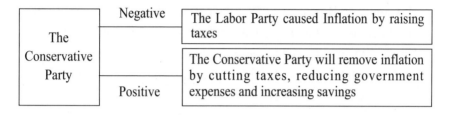

The Conservative Party	Negative	The Labor Party caused Inflation by raising taxes
	Positive	The Conservative Party will remove inflation by cutting taxes, reducing government expenses and increasing savings

Hanara in government, Candidate Daejung Kim of Party Kookmin Council in opposition, and Candidate Injae Lee of Party Kookminshindang in opposition. The three candidates' strong points were integrity for Canidate Hoichang Lee, plenty of experience in politics for Candidate Daejung Kim, and vigor due to youth for Candidate Injae Lee. In the meantime, the three candidates' weak points were insufficient experience in politics for Candidate Hoichang Lee, too old and untrustworthy for Candidate Daejung Kim, and insufficient experience and untrustworthy for Candidate Injae Lee.

Figure 3.2 *Comparative strategies* **of the 1997 presidential election in Korea**

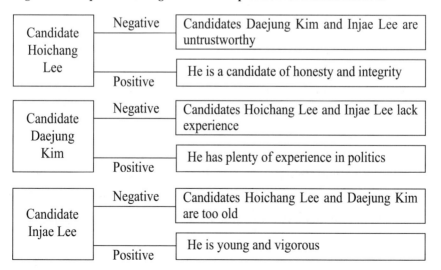

Candidate Hoichang Lee	Negative	Candidates Daejung Kim and Injae Lee are untrustworthy
	Positive	He is a candidate of honesty and integrity
Candidate Daejung Kim	Negative	Candidates Hoichang Lee and Injae Lee lack experience
	Positive	He has plenty of experience in politics
Candidate Injae Lee	Negative	Candidates Hoichang Lee and Daejung Kim are too old
	Positive	He is young and vigorous

As seen in Figure 3.2, all three candidates used *comparative strategies* and made a catchphrase based on them.

① Candidate Hoichang Lee's catchphrase was "a candidate of honesty and integrity" in order to contrast himself from his opponents, Daejung Kim and Injae Lee, whom voters did not trust.

② Candidate Daejung Kim's catchphrase was "a candidate of experience" in order to contrast himself from his opponents, Hoichang Lee and Injae Lee who lacked experience.

③ Candidate Injae Lee's catchphrase was "a candidate full of youth and vigor," in order to contrast himself from his opponents, Daejung Kim and Hoichang Lee's old age.

5. *Responsive Strategies*

These strategies are about how to respond to the opponents' criticism. A candidate who does not properly respond to criticism of him/herself is likely to lose in an election for the following reasons.

① Voters cannot have favorable feelings toward a candidate who does not appropriately respond to criticism of him/herself.

② The mass media tends to intensively report negative criticism when a candidate fails to properly respond to criticism of him/herself.

③ If a candidate fails to appropriately respond at the time when the criticism of him/herself begins, he/she repeatedly exposes his/her criticized weak points and also loses the opportunity to fulfill his/her own strategies.

④ Once a candidate loses support because of inappropriate response to criticism of him/herself, it is very difficult for him/her to regain that lost support. Particularly, it is almost impossible for a candidate to regain the lost support in an election in which the campaign period is short, like 1-2 months.

⑤ A candidate who cannot respond well to criticism of him/herself cannot receive many donations, because the candidate projects the image of a loser.

6. Interrelations among the Five Strategies

A candidate who corrects his/her weak points before the campaign begins does not need to prepare responses to criticism of him/herself, because his/her opponents cannot use *negative strategies* or *comparative strategies* against him/her. In this case, as seen in Figure 3.3, his/her opponents have no choice but to use *positive strategies* that are usually regarded as the most ineffective.

Figure 3.3 Interrelations between strategies

As Figure 3.4 shows, a candidate who fails to make up for his/her weak points naturally becomes a subject of *negative strategies* or *comparative strategies* among his/her opponents. Then, he/she has to *use responsive strategies;* consequently, he/she is easily put into a defensive position.

Figure 3.4 Interrelations among strategies

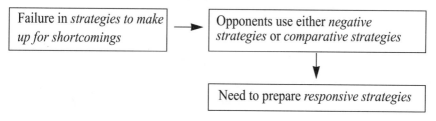

7. Proper Strategies under Different Circumstances

The strategies a candidate should choose under a certain circumstance are as follows.

① When a candidate is far behind his/her opponents in candidate support and when the number of the undecided voters is very small, he/she can win by considerably curtailing support for his/her opponents. Therefore, he/she must use *negative strategies* or *comparative strategies*.

② When a candidate is far ahead of his/her opponents in support and, when the number of the undecided voters is very small, he/she can win by sustaining or increasing current support. Therefore, it is better for him/her to use *positive strategies*.

8. Most Frequently Used Strategies by Candidates in Korea

Candidates in Korea usually do not believe that it is very crucial to use *strategies to make up for their shortcomings*. As a result, they are negligent about using *strategies to make up for their shortcomings*. In the meantime, they think that *negative-and comparative strategies* against their opponents are very crucial to their success in the election. As a result, most candidates focus on *negative or comparative strategies* against their opponents, so the election always looks muddy to voters.

Chapter 4

Target Voters

It may not be true that all voters contribute equally to a candidate's victory. There are voters who can help a candidate win, whereas there are ones who help very little with their vote. Efforts to get support from the latter are only a waste of time and resources. Therefore, first of all, a candidate and his/her staff must discriminate between voters who can directly affect the candidate's victory and voters who don't matter. The former group of voters is called *target voters* whose support a candidate must eagerly ask for in order to win.

The following examples offer two opposite strategies regarding *target voters*.[11] Republican Richard Nixon attempted to catch all votes by vowing to visit every state in the 1960 presidential election in the United States. His problem was that he wasted a large amount of his time and resources by visiting states where he had already won or lost, regardless of his visit. In the end, he was defeated by John F. Kennedy in one of the closest presidential elections in American history. In contrast, Democrat Bill Clinton in the 1992 presidential election in the United States sorted states into three categories:ones they never could win, ones they would win, and toss-up

---

[11] Shea, *Campaign Craft*, 71.

states. He then proceeded to spend no effort on states in the first two categories, but concentrated his campaign efforts on the toss-up states, and won the election.

1. Reasons for Setting up *Target Voters*

There are three reasons for setting up *target voters*.

①The campaign period is not long enough, so the candidate cannot get in touch with all voters to ask for their votes. Therefore, the candidate must maximize his/her winning probability by setting up *target voters* who help him/her win easily and then, intensively asking them to vote for him/her.

② *Target voters* clearly indicate which voters a candidate and his/her canvassers must contact during the campaign period.

③ Candidates can bring up appropriate issues and policies in order to get votes effectively only after setting up *target voters*.

2. Methods for Setting up *Target Voters*

There are two methods for setting up *target voters*. The first method is based on the results of previous elections in the district. The second method is based on the results of a private survey conducted by pollsters working for a candidate.

(1) Setting up *Target Voters* based on the Results of Previous Elections

These methods are divided into two: (a) the method to set up *target voters* based on the results of the most recent election and (b) the method to set up *target voters* based on the results of multiple elections in the past. Both methods are based on the same assumption that *straight-ticket voters* are not proper targets for any candidate's campaign, because they are likely to vote for the party that they prefer, regardless of who is a candidate of the party and how well the candidate campaigns. Therefore, candidates must select their *target voters* among *split-ticket voters* who cast their votes based on comparing the qualities of candidates.

These methods are less accurate, but cost much less than the method based on the results of a private survey. Therefore, candidates who do not have sufficient funds may use these methods first.

(a) Setting up *Target Voters* based on the Results of the Most Recent Election

In the following, this method is explained with an assumed district. As seen in Figure 4.1, the assumed district is composed of six precincts, and only two candidates, A and B, from two political parties are in competition.

The criterion of analysis is the line of an angle of 45 degrees as seen in Figure 4.1. It is assumed that the closer a precinct is to the line, the more *split-ticket voters* there must be in that precinct who would be likely to shift their support. Therefore, it would be wise for candidates to select those voters who live closer to the line as their *target voters*. In fact, the author has observed that the closer the competition between the candidates in a precinct, the more voters are likely to be "on the fence" and the more voters are likely to shift their support in that precinct.

Among the six precincts in Figure 4.1, Precincts 3, 4, 5, and 6 are prime targets, because they are almost equally closer to the line than the other two Precincts, 1 and 2.

Precincts 3 and 4 are quite different from Precincts 5 and 6. In the former

Figure 4.1 Results of the most recent election

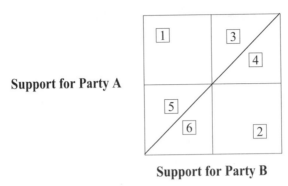

Support for Party B

precincts, support for both parties is high, while support for all other parties and independent candidates is very low. In the latter precincts, support for both parties is low, while support for all other parties or independent candidates is very high. Consequently, when strong independent candidates or candidates from third parties come forward, the targets of high priority among the four precincts would be Precincts 3 and 4. In the meantime, when weak independent candidates or candidates from third parties run, their main targets would be Precincts 5 and 6.

If all conditions are the same as to matters described so far, target precincts are decided based on the population density and facility of contact with voters. A precinct with the highest population density and in which candidates are able to contact voters most easily will be a target of the highest priority.

However, the method of setting up *target voters* based on the results of the most recent election is not recommended to be used in the following two cases. The first is when the most recent election is not one of typical elections held in the district, because it cannot be a criterion for a candidate to set up targets for the forthcoming election. The second is when a district is composed of groups that are seriously conflicted with each other, and almost all voters belong to one of these groups or another.

(b) Setting up *Target Voters* based on the Results of Multiple Elections in the Past

These methods include the following: analysis of *split-ticket voters* and analysis of *non-fixed supporters* for parties. Both methods are the same, in that they attempt to measure the number of voters who shifted their support from one party to another in past elections.

(b.1) Analysis of *Split-Ticket Voters*

This method compares the results of more than two elections in the past. It calculates the number of *split-ticket voters* who shifted their support from one party to another in order to select them as the *target voters* for the present campaign.[12] As seen below, the number of *split-ticket voters* is calculated by subtracting the minimum number of votes from the maximum number of votes obtained by a party in previous elections. The more ticket splitters there are in a precinct, the greater target that precinct will be.

■ Formula of an Analysis of the *Split-Ticket Voters*

Number of *split-ticket voters* for each precinct = (Maximum number of votes obtained by a party in previous elections for each precinct) - (Minimum number of votes obtained by the party in the previous elections for each precinct)

Table 4.1 illustrates an assumed example of an *analysis of split-ticket voters* for a district composed of four precincts, A, B, C, and D, based on three different elections: the presidential election, the congressional election, and the mayoral election.

For Precinct A, since a party obtained maximum number of votes in the

---

[12] An analysis of *swing voters* is based on the number of voters who shift their support from one party to another in elections held in different periods. An analysis of *split-ticket voters* is based on the number of voters who shift their support for one party at one level of election to support for another party at another level of election in elections held at the same time. However, since the principle of both analyses is the same, they are all referred to as "analysis of *split-ticket voters*" in this book.

presidential election and minimum number of votes in the congressional election, the number of the ticket splitters of Precinct A is 25%. For each of the other three precincts, the number of the ticket splitters is calculated in the same way. The target precinct is therefore ordered as follows: A, B, C, and D.

Table 4.1 The number of *split-ticket voters*

Precinct	Presidential Election	Congressional Election	Mayoral Election	Number of split-ticket voters (ranking)
A	20%	45%	35%	45-20=25%(1)
B	40%	30%	50%	50-30=20%(2)
C	30%	35%	40%	40-30=10%(3)
D	40%	35%	40%	40-35=5%(4)

There are three differences between an analysis of *split-ticket voters* and an analysis based on the most recent election.

① The former is based on a comparison of votes received by a party in more than two elections, while the latter is based on a comparison of votes obtained by different parties in an election. Hence, a party's target precincts could be different in the two analyses.

② In the analysis of the *split-ticket voters*, the number of voters shifting their support is considerably evident, whereas in the analysis based on the most recent election, the number of voters shifting their support is only estimated.

Notable points in using the analysis of the *split-ticket voters* are as follows:

① The analysis of the *split-ticket voters* can be used only when the composition of parties that nominate candidates is the same in at least two elections. For example, if two candidates from Parties A and B competed in one election and only candidates from those two parties also contested in the other election, a ticket splitter analysis can be used based on the results of these two elections. In other words, if only two candidates from Parties A and B competed in one election and two candidates from Parties A and B plus an independent candidate contested in the other election, the analysis of the *split-ticket voters* cannot be used based on the results of the two elections.

② If possible, a ticket splitter analysis must be conducted based on the results of recent elections. It may not be appropriate to do a ticket splitter analysis based on the results of elections held more than 10 years ago.

Districts in which the Analysis of the *Split-Ticket Voters* is Accurate

The more *straight-ticket voters* there are in a district, that is, those who vote for a candidate based on their evaluation of the party nominating the candidate rather than their evaluation of that candidate, the more accurate is the analysis of the *split-ticket voters*.

For example, as seen in Table 4.2, in the district composed of only four voters, all voters are *straight-ticket voters* and they have supported the same party in two successive elections. In this case, the real number of *split-ticket voters* based on two elections is 0% for both parties, which is exactly the same as the numerical value calculated by using the formula of the analysis of *split-ticket voters*. In detail, the number of the *split-ticket voters* of Party A is 0% (75% - 75%), as is the number of the *split-ticket voters* of Party B (25% -25%).

Table 4.2 Case in which the real number of *split-ticket voters* and the number of *plit-ticket voters* obtained through the formula are the same

Voter	Election 1		Election 2	
	Party A	Party B	Party A	Party B
Voter 1	X		X	
Voter 2	X		X	
Voter 3	X		X	
Voter 4		X		X
Total (100%)	3 (75%)	1 (25%)	3 (75%)	1 (25%)

Districts in which the Analysis of the *Split-Ticket Voters* is not Accurate

The more *split-ticket voters* there are in a district - that is, the more voters who vote for a candidate based on their own evaluation of the candidate rather than their evaluation of the party nominating that candidate - the less accurate is the analysis of the *split-ticket voters*. For example, as seen in Table 4.3, in the district composed of only four voters, all voters have supported a different party in two consecutive elections, because they are all *split-ticket voters*. In detail, Voters 1 and 2 supported Party A in one election, while they cast votes for Party B in the next election. Voters 3 and 4 supported Party B in one election, while they cast votes for Party A in the next election. Therefore, the real number of *split-ticket voters* for both Parties A and B should be 100%.

However, the number of the *split-ticket voters* of each party calculated with the formula is 0% (50% - 50%), which is entirely wrong. Then, it is very risky to use the analysis of the *split-ticket voters* in a district where the majority of voters are *split-ticket voters*.

Table 4.3 Case in which the real number of *split-ticket voters* and the number of *split-ticket voters* obtained through the formula are directly opposite

Voter	Election 1		Election 2	
	Party A	Party B	Party A	Party B
Voter 1	X			X
Voter 2	X			X
Voter 3		X	X	
Voter 4		X	X	
Total (100%)	2 (50%)	2 (50%)	2 (50%)	2 (50%)

(b.2) Analysis of Aggregate *Non-Fixed Supporters* for Parties[13]

This method compares the results of more than two previous elections to calculate the number of *non-fixed supporters* for parties who shifted their support from one party to another. The higher the number of *non-fixed supporters* for parties that a precinct has, the greater target that precinct becomes in the district.

The number of *fixed supporters* for each party is estimated by the sum of the worst number of votes that each party obtained in recent elections. *Non-fixed supporters* are calculated by subtracting the sum of *fixed supporters* for parties from the number of total voters. Then, if only two political parties, A and B, are competing in an election, the formula would be as follows.

■ Formula of the Analysis of Aggregate *Non-Fixed Supporters* for Parties

Number of *non-fixed supporters* for parties for each precinct = Total voters for each precinct - *fixed supporters* for Party A for each precinct (Minimum number of votes obtained by Party A in previous elections for each precinct) - *fixed supporters* for Party B for each precinct (Minimum number of votes obtained by Party B in previous elections for each precinct)

(2) Setting up Target based on the Results of a Private Survey

Five kinds of targets can be set up based on the results of a private survey, including (a) *target for raising recognition*, (b) *target voters*, (c) *target opponent* and (d) *target for increasing supporters' voting rate*.

(a) *Target for Raising Recognition*

Split-ticket voters never vote for a candidate whom they do not recognize. Therefore, a candidate has to find voters who do not recognize him/herself

---

[13] It is also called "aggregate base-vote analysis," See Shea, *Campaign Craft*, 86.

and make them recognize him/herself. Then, a certain candidate's *target for raising recognition* includes voters who do not recognize him/herself. The following points are important when considering whether to campaign to get recognized.

① Setting up *target for raising recognition* is not necessary for all candidates. If voters' recognition of a candidate is over 90%, the candidate does not need to establish *target for raising recognition*.

② A candidate's getting recognition from voters does not necessarily mean obtaining support. Therefore, campaigning to raise recognition must be completed in the early stages of the campaign period. In the middle and last stages, the candidate must make an effort to get support from voters.

When setting up target to get recognized, the following criteria must be met.

A candidate's prime *target for raising recognition* is those voters who would probably support the candidate by just getting to recognize him/her. These kinds of voters are described below.

ⓐ **Voters who recognize the opponents but do not support them**

If the candidate is successful in giving even a slightly good impression of him/herself to voters who know his/her opponents but do not support them, he/she would be likely to get support from those voters.

ⓑ **Voters living in precincts where he/she gets stronger support than his/her opponents**

Since these voters are surrounded by supporters for the candidate, it is highly possible that favorable oral transmission for the candidate from his/her supporters will reach these voters to give them a good impression of him/herself.

ⓒ **Voters who live in precincts in which there are many *split-ticket voters***

A candidate can raise support for him/herself much with increasing voters' recognition of him/herself in a district where most of the voters are *split-ticket voters*.

The process of setting up *target for raising recognition* is not simple, because various surrounding variables must be simultaneously considered. Particularly, the process is very complex in an election in which many candidates compete.

The *target for raising recognition* is usually set up by the distinction of sex, age, or precinct. Target by sex or age is usually useful for public relations materials, media events and campaigning for support from groups. Target by precinct is generally helpful to a candidate's contact with individual voters.

Following are two hypothetical examples of setting up *target for raising recognition* by precinct under the simplest circumstances.

Example I
① Condition
- A district is composed of three precincts (X, Y, Z). Population densities and the number of voters in the three precincts are almost the same.
- Only two candidates, A and B, are in competition. Voters' recognition of both candidates is the same at 50% of the total voters.
- Both candidates are almost the same in support for themselves. However, support for them in each precinct is not all the same. Candidate A leads Candidate B in support by 10% in Precinct X. Support for both candidates is almost the same in Precinct Y. Candidate B leads Candidate A in support by 10% in Precinct Z.
- The number of undecided voters is the same at 50% in all three precincts.
② Candidate A's *target for raising recognition*
- Candidate A's primary target is Precinct Y. Since two candidates are in very close competition in this district, a candidate who beats off his/her competitor in Precinct Y could win.
- Candidate A's second target is Precinct X. Since Candidate A has stronger support than Candidate B in this precinct, it is highly possible

that favorable oral transmission for Candidate A from his/her supporters to the undecided voters is stronger than in the other two precincts. Consequently, Candidate A can raise support for him/herself easily by increasing voters' recognition of him/herself in Precinct X.

- Candidate A's third target is Precinct Z. Since Candidate A has weaker support than Candidate B in this precinct, it is probable that favorable oral transmission for Candidate A from his/her supporters to the undecided voters is the weakest among the three precincts. As a result, it is difficult for Candidate A to increase support for him/herself by increasing voters' recognition of him/herself in Precinct Z.

③ Candidate B's *target for raising recognition*

- By the same logic as seen in the process of setting up Candidate A's *target for raising recognition*, Candidate B's prime target is Precinct Y, the second target is Precinct Z, and the third target is Precinct X.

Table 4.4 Voters' recognition of each candidate

	Precinct X	Precinct Y	Precinct Z	Total
Candidate A	60%	50%	40%	50%
Candidate B	70%	80%	90%	80%

Example II

① Conditions

- A district is composed of three precincts (X, Y, Z). Population densities and number of voters in the three precincts are almost the same.

- Only two candidates, A and B, are in competition. As Table 4.4 shows, 50% of the total voters recognizes Candidate A and 80% of the total voters recognizes Candidate B. However, voters' recognition of each candidate is different from precinct to precinct. Voters' recognition of Candidate A is 60% in Precinct X, 50% in Precinct Y, and 40% in Precinct Z. Meanwhile, voters' recognition of Candidate B is 70% in

Precinct X, 80% in Precinct Y, and 90% in Precinct Z.

- Support for both candidates is the same at 25% in all precincts. The number of undecided voters is also the same at 50% in all three precincts.

②Candidate A's *target for raising recognition*

- Candidate A's prime target is Precinct Z. In detail, while other conditions such as support for candidates and the number of undecided voters are the same in all three precincts, voters' recognition of Candidate A is the lowest and voters' recognition of Candidate B is the highest in Precinct Z. This means that most of the undecided voters in Precinct Z do not intend to vote for Candidate B, because they do not show their support for Candidate B, in spite of the fact that 90% of them already recognizes Candidate B. This fact implies that when Candidate A raises voters' recognition of him/herself in Precinct Z, he/she increases his/her support most effectively.

- Candidate A's second target is Precinct Y. The reason is that while this precinct is the same as other precincts in support for candidates and the number of undecided voters, it is second in both voters' recognition of Candidates A and B.

- Candidate A's third target is Precinct X. The reason is that while this precinct is the same in support for candidates and the number of undecided voters as in other precincts, it is lowest in voters' recognition of Candidate B and highest in voters' recognition of Candidate A.

③Candidate B's *target for raising recognition*

- Candidate B's prime target is Precinct X. This precinct is the lowest among the three precincts in voters' recognition of Candidate B, other conditions, such as support for candidates and the number of decided voters being the same in all three precincts. This means that when Candidate B raises voters' recognition of him/herself in this district, he/she increases support for him/herself most effectively.

- Candidate B's second target is Precinct Y. The reason is that this precinct is the same as other precincts in the number of undecided voters and support for candidates, while it is second in ranking in voters' recognition of Candidate B.

- Precinct Z cannot even be a *target for raising recognition* for Candidate B. The reason is that since voters' recognition for Candidate B is already 90% in this precinct, it is difficult to expect a rise of voters' recognition of the candidate any more.

(b) *Target Voters*

This is concerned with whom a candidate should contact in order to win. Voters are divided into four types, *fixed supporters, fluid supporters*, undecided voters, and *indifferent voters*. The characteristics of each type and the relationship that each type has with the *target voters* are described below.

Fixed supporters are those who very strongly support a certain candidate because they favor the candidate's party or the candidate's image or career. Consequently, it is almost impossible for any candidate to convert his/her opponents' *fixed supporters* to support him/herself. Usually, any attempt to convert other candidates' *fixed supporters* is only a waste of time and resources. *Fixed supporters* are easily found among *straight-ticket voters* rather than *split-ticket voters*, because the former is more intense in strength of support than the latter.

Fixed supporters tend to do a great deal of favorable oral transmission about the candidate they support to other voters. Therefore, a candidate who has more *fixed supporters* than his/her opponents occupies a stronger position in a campaign. It allows him/her to attack the opponent easily, making his/her opponents' attack on him/herself difficult. If a candidate's *fixed supporters* are more than 50% of the total voters, he/she can never lose the election under any circumstances.

Fluid supporters are those who are favorable to a certain candidate because they like the candidate's party or the candidate's image or career. However, they can switch and support other candidates if the situation changes. In one word, *fluid supporters* are weak supporters for a candidate.

Undecided voters are those who have not decided whom to support yet. They are divided into two types. The first type includes those who do not have enough information yet about all of the candidates. A candidate can get their support by providing them with positive information about him/herself and with negative information about his/her opponents.

The second type includes those who prefer more than two candidates and have not yet decided on which candidate they will support. A candidate can get their support from the second type only when he/she successfully persuades them with acceptable reasons to support him/herself.

Indifferent voters are a type of *undecided voters*. However, they are different from *undecided voters*, in that they are not interested in elections at all. As a matter of fact, *indifferent voters* are never subjects of a campaign because it is very difficult for candidates to reach them. Even if they were contacted by candidates or canvassers, they may not remember whom it was that they met. Therefore, it is not recommended that a candidate select *indifferent voters* as *target voters*.

Indifferent voters usually have two particular characteristics. First, most of them avoid going to the voting booth on Election Day. Second, if *indifferent voters* go to the polls, it is very difficult to predict for whom they might vote.

They tend to vote based on information and evaluations concerning political parties obtained from family members or mass media just before voting. Hence, indifferent voters are particularly unfavorable to unknown independent candidates and candidates of small parties to whom the mass media has paid little attention. In an election when the number of *indifferent voters* is great, candidate support can vary rapidly just before Election Day, since *indifferent voters* choose a candidate to support just a few days before Election Day.

    (b.1) Criteria for Setting up *Target Voters*

       ① If a candidate is far ahead of others in support and can win with support from only his/her fixed and *fluid supporters*, his/her *target voters* are his/her *fluid supporters*. In detail, the candidate's *fluid supporters* will be the main targets of his/her opponents, because they may change their support more easily than his/her *fixed supporters*. Therefore, the candidate should focus on protecting his/her *fluid supporters* from attack of his/her opponents.

       ② If there is little difference in support among candidates, a candidate's prime *target voters* are undecided voters and the second *target voters* are his/her *fluid supporters*. In detail, first of all, each candidate must try to obtain support from the undecided voters. If the candidate is successful in getting support from the undecided voters, his/her next step must be to focus on protecting his/her *fluid supporters* from attack of his/her opponents.

       ③ If a candidate is far behind others in support and cannot win with support from all undecided voters, a candidate's prime *target voters* are his/her opponents' *fluid supporters* and the second *target voters* are undecided voters. First of all, this candidate must put all his/her efforts into converting his/her opponents' fluid supporters into his/her own supporters. Then, if these efforts turn out to be successful, the candidate's next step must be to attempt to get support from the undecided voters.

    (b.2) Possibility of Success, Time and Resources Required, and Change in Support

Depending on who the *target voters* are, attack on a target may require different amounts of time and resources, and may result in different rates of success and different degrees of change in support, as seen in Table 4.5.

① If a candidate's prime *target voters* are his/her *fluid supporters*, the possibility of the success in protecting them from the opponents' attack is high, and the time and amount of resources required is the least. However, although the effort to sustain the support of *fluid supporters* is successful, radical change in support cannot be expected.

② If a candidate's prime *target voters* are his/her opponents' *fluid supporters*, the possibility of success in attacking them is low, and the time and amount of resources required is the largest. However, if the attack is successful, radical change in support is expected.

③ If a candidate's prime *target voters* are undecided voters, the possibility of success in getting their support, the time and amount of resources required, and scope of change in support caused by successfully getting the votes of undecided voters is between the two cases above.

Table 4.5 The types of targets and possibility of success, time and resources required, and degree of change in support

Target	Possibility of success	Time required	Amount of resources required	Change in support
Candidate's fluid supporters	High	Short	Little	Small
Undecided voters	Middle	Middle	Middle	Middle
Opponents' fluid supporters	Low	Long	Much	Big

(b.3) Hypothetical Examples of *Target Voters*

Target voters are set up by sex, age, or precinct. Target set up by age or sex is useful mainly for campaigning through the mass media and pamphlets, and campaigning on groups. Target by precinct is useful for the candidate and his/her canvassers to make direct contact with individual voters. Two hypothetical examples of setting up *target voters* by precinct under the simplest conditions are as follows.

Example I
① Conditions
The district is composed of three precincts (X, Y, Z). The number of voters and population density are the same in all three precincts. Competition is between Candidates A and B who have the same score at 80% of the total voters in voters' recognition of them.

As seen in Table 4.6, support for Candidate A is 55% of the total voters. Of these, 25% is *fixed supporters* and 30% is *fluid supporters*. Meanwhile, support for Candidate B is 30% of the total voters. One half of 30% is *fixed supporters* and the other half is *fluid supporters*. The number of undecided voters amounts to 15% of the total voters. The following is the distribution of voters by precinct.

- Out of Candidate A's *fixed supporters*, 40% is in Precinct X; 35% in Precinct Y; and 25% in Precinct Z. Out of Candidate A's *fluid supporters*, 40% is in Precinct X; 35% in Precinct Y; and 25% in Precinct Z.

- Out of Candidate B's *fixed supporters*, 25% is in Precinct X; 35% in Precinct Y; and 40% in Precinct Z. Out of Candidate B's *fluid supporters*, 25% is in Precinct X; 35% in Precinct Y; and 40% in Precinct Z.

- Out of the undecided voters, 25% is in Precinct X; 35% in Precinct Y; and 40% in Precinct Z.

Table 4.6 Distribution of voters by precinct

Candidate A						Candidate B						Undecided voter		
Support: 55%						Support: 30%						15%		
Fixed supporter 25%			Fluid supporter 30%			Fixed supporter 15%			Fluid supporter 15%					
Precinct			Precinct			Precinct			Precinct			Precinct		
X	Y	Z	X	Y	Z	X	Y	Z	X	Y	Z	X	Y	Z
40	35	25	40	35	25	25	35	40	25	35	40	25	35	40

②Candidate A's *Target Voters*

The sum of Candidate A's *fixed* and *fluid supporters* is 55% of the total voters. Therefore, Candidate A's prime target includes his/her *fluid supporters*. That is, Candidate A must do his/her best to keep his/her *fluid supporters* from his/her opponent's attack on them. Once Candidate A is successful in keeping his/her *fluid supporters* early in a campaign, he/she must continue to make an effort to not to lose his/her *fluid supporters* up to Election Day. If Candidate A fails to keep his/her *fluid supporters*, he/she makes an effort to get support from the undecided voters as the next step.

By precinct, Precinct X is Candidate A's prime target, because it has the largest number of his/her *fluid supporters* among the three precincts; Precinct Y is the second target, because it is in the middle in the number of his/her *fluid supporters*; Precinct Z is the third, because it has the least number of his/her *fluid supporters*.

③Candidate B's *Target Voters*

The sum of Candidate B's *fixed* and *fluid supporters* and the undecided voters is only 45% of the total voters. Therefore, Candidate B must get support from Candidate A's *fluid supporters* in order to win; then, his/her prime target is Candidate A's *fluid supporters*. If Candidate B is successful in getting support from Candidate A's *fluid supporters,* he/she must try to obtain support from undecided voters as the next step.

By precinct, Precinct X is Candidate B's prime target, because it has the largest number of Candidate A's *fluid supporters* among the three precincts; Precinct Y is the second target, because it is in the middle in the number of Candidate A's *fluid supporters*; Precinct Z is the third, because it has the least number of Candidate A's *fluid supporters*.

Example II

① Conditions

The district is composed of three precincts (X, Y, Z). The number of voters and population density are the same in all three precincts. The competition is between Candidates A and B who have the same score at 80% of the total voters in voters' recognition of them.

As seen in Table 4.7, Candidate A's supporters amount to 40%. Out of these, half is *fixed supporters* and the other half is *fluid supporters.* Meanwhile, Candidate B's supporters amount to 30%, out of which 20% is *fixed supporters* and 10% is *fluid supporters.* Undecided voters amount to 30%.

Table 4.7 Distribution of voters by precinct

Candidate A						Candidate B						Undecided voter		
Support: 40%						Support: 30%						30%		
Fixed supporter 20%			Fluid supporter 20%			Fixed supporter 20%			Fluid supporter 10%					
Precinct			Precinct			Precinct			Precinct			Precinct		
X	Y	Z	X	Y	Z	X	Y	Z	X	Y	Z	X	Y	Z
40	35	25	40	35	25	25	35	40	25	35	40	25	35	40

The following is the distribution of voters by precinct.

- Out of Candidate A's *fixed supporters*, 40% is in Precinct X; 35% in Precinct Y; and 25% in Precinct Z. Out of Candidate A's *fluid supporters*, 40% is in Precinct X; 35% in Precinct Y; and 25% in Precinct Z.

- Out of Candidate B' *fixed supporters*, 25% is in Precinct X; 35% in Precinct Y; and 40% in Precinct Z. Out of Candidate B's *fluid supporters*, 25% is in Precinct X; 35% in Precinct Y; and 40% in Precinct Z.

- Out of undecided voters, 25% is in Precinct X; 35% in Precinct Y; and 40% in Precinct Z.

② Candidate A's *Target Voters*

Although Candidate A is ahead of Candidate B by 10% in support, he/she cannot be sure that he/she will win, because the number of undecided voters still amounts to 30% of the total voters. Therefore, Candidate A's prime target is comprised of undecided voters. If Candidate A is successful in getting support from more than half of the undecided voters, he/she must keep his/her *fluid supporters* from his/her opponent's attack on them as the next step. However, if Candidate A fails to get the support of almost all undecided voters, he/she must attempt to convert Candidate B's *fluid supporters* to his/her supporters as the next step.

By precinct, Precinct Z is Candidate A's prime target, because it has the largest number of undecided voters among the three precincts; Precinct Y is the second target, because it is in the middle in the number of undecided voters; Precinct Z is the third target, because it has the least number of undecided voters.

③ Candidate B's *Target Voters*

Although Candidate B is behind Candidate A by 10% in support, he/she can still win if he/she is successful in getting support from the most undecided voters. Therefore, Candidate B's prime target is the undecided voters. If Candidate B is successful in getting support from the most undecided voters, he/she must try to keep his/her *fluid supporters* from his/her opponent's attack on them. However, if Candidate B fails in getting support from undecided voters, he/she must attack Candidate A's *fluid supporters* to get their support.

By precincts, Precinct Z is Candidate B's prime target because it has the largest number of undecided voters among the three precincts; Precinct Y is the second, because it is in the middle in the number of undecided voters; Precinct X is the third, because it has the least number of undecided voters.

(c) *Target Opponent*

A candidate must make voters acknowledge his/her opponents' defects to curtail support for them. When there are only two candidates, it is evident who is the main opponent. However, when there are more than three candidates, a candidate must decide whom to especially attack. That is, an opponent whom a candidate must principally attack is the *target opponent*. The following suggests two criteria for identifying a *target opponent*.

① A candidate's target must be one of his/her opponents who is the most similar to him/her in significant characteristics. Then, if he/she is successful in attacking that opponent, the opponent's supporters who are disappointed with the opponent would be likely to support him/her rather than the other opponents.

② If the characteristics of all candidates are very similar, a candidate must attack an opponent whose supporters' strength of support is the weakest, since it would be difficult to be successful in attacking an opponent whose supporters' strength of support is very strong.

Table 4.8 Criteria for deciding on a *target opponent*

		Degree of similarity of characteristics between a candidate and his/her opponent	
		High	Low
Strength of support	Weak	Prime target (1)	Second target (2)
	Strong	Second target (3)	Third target (4)

Table 4.8 shows the ranks of *target opponents*, considering the two criteria described above at the same time. A candidate's prime target (1) is an opponent who has very similar characteristics to him/herself and also whose supporters' strength of support is weak.

The second target can either be the opponent (2) who has very different characteristics from him/her, but whose supporters' strength of support is weak or the opponent (3) who has very similar characteristics to him/her but whose supporters' strength of support is strong. If the purpose of attack is just to curtail support for the attacked opponent, while not getting support from the opponent's supporters, the former (2) is prior to the latter (3). If the purpose of attack is to convert supporters of the attacked opponent to support him/herself, the latter (3) is prior to the former (2).

The third target is the opponent (4) who has very different characteristics from the candidate and whose supporters' strength of support is the strongest.

Table 4.9 Case of the 1997 presidential election in Korea

Candidate	Strength of support	Opponent with similar characteristics
Daejung Kim	Strong	None
Hoichang Lee	Middle	Injae Lee
Injae Lee	Weak	Hoichang Lee

Table 4.9 shows the characteristics of candidates in the 1997 presidential election in Korea and supporters' strength of support for each candidate. The strength of support for Candidate Daejung Kim was the strongest and his characteristics were not similar to any other candidate's. The strength of support for Candidate Hoichang Lee was in the middle and his characteristics were similar to Candidate Injae Lee. The strength of support for Candidate Injae Lee was the weakest and his characteristics were similar to Candidate Hoichang Lee. Under these conditions, a *target opponent* of each was as follows.

①No other candidate had similar characteristics to Daejung Kim. Then, Daejung Kim's prime target was Injae Lee, who was the weakest in strength of support. However, a successful attack on Injae Lee by Daejung Kim would make supporters for Injae Lee support Hoichang Lee rather than Daejung Kim. Therefore, when Hoichang Lee was far ahead of the other two in support, Daejung Kim's prime *target opponent* had to be Hoichang Lee.

② Hoichang Lee's prime *target opponent* was Injae Lee because Injae Lee had similar characteristics to him and the strength of support for Injae Lee was the weakest. Hoichang Lee's second *target opponent* was Daejung Kim.

③ Injae Lee's prime *target opponent* was Hoichang Lee, because Hoichang Lee had similar characteristics to him and strength of support for Hoichang Lee was in the middle. His second *target opponent* was Daejung Kim.

(d) *Target for Increasing Supporters' Voting Rate*

(d.1) Reasons of Setting up *Target for Increasing Supporters' Voting Rate*

Although a candidate is ahead of his/her opponents in support, he/she cannot win if his/her supporters do not go to the polling booth. Therefore, a candidate does his/her best to raise his/her supporters' voting rate 4 to 5 days before an election. For this, the candidate needs to set up *target for increasing supporters' voting rate*.

However, the opportunity to raise supporters' voting rate is given to all candidates. A candidate, who is far behind others in support, makes an effort to get more votes even up to Election Day, rather than 'making an effort to raise the supporters' voting rate.

(d.2) Criteria for Setting up *Target for Increasing Supporters' Voting Rate*

The *target for increasing supporters' voting rate* is mainly those who are likely not to go to the polling booth. Then, the supporters' strength of support and the degree of the supporters' intention to go to the polls are usually simultaneously considered.

① The stronger the supporters' strength of support, the more probable it is that they will go to the polls. The voting rate of *fixed supporters* is higher than that of *fluid supporters*. Therefore, *fluid supporters* are the prime target.

② Supporters, who do not think that going to the polls is their obligation, should be the prime target. Their numbers are greater among the younger-, less-educated-, lower-income-, and urban residents.

Table 4.10 Criteria for deciding on a *target for increasing supporters' voting rate*

		Do you think voting is an obligation?	
		No	Yes
Strength of support	Low	Prime target	Second target
	High	Second target	Third target

Table 4.10 indicates the ranks of the target, considering the two criteria described above at the same time.

① A candidate's prime target is his/her supporters whose strength of support is low and who do not think that they are obligated to go to the polling booth.

② A candidate's second target may be of two kinds. One is his/her supporters whose strength of support is high, but who do not think that they are obligated to go to the polling booth. The other is his/her supporters whose strength of support is low, and who believe that they are obligated to go to the polling booth.

③ A candidate's third target is his/her supporters whose strength of support is high and who believe that they are obligated to go to the polling booth.

(d.3) How to Raise Supporters' Voting Rates

① Grasp supporters' strength of support, age, and attainment in scholarship, and obtain their telephone number.

② Classify supporters into the first, second and third targets based on information about supporters.

③ From 4 to 5 days before Election Day, systematically attempt to call and visit targets by asking them to go to the polling booth.

(e) *Target for Oral Transmission*

Oral transmission about the election and candidates among voters is an invisible, but most crucial factor in the election, because it strongly influences voters' behavior. Therefore, a candidate must make a tremendous effort to spread favorable oral transmission about him/herself and unfavorable oral transmission about his/her opponents to voters by setting up *target for oral transmission*.

(e.1) Criteria for Setting up *Target for Oral Transmission*

Target for oral transmission can be set up by precinct, age, time, or income and academic attainment. The following is criteria for target by each of the above.

Criteria for Setting up *Target for Oral Transmission* by Precinct

① A candidate must begin oral transmission in the precinct where he/she has stronger support than his/her opponents. More specifically, in the precinct where the candidate's supporters are greater in number than his/her opponents', oral transmission for him/her is easily transmitted by his/her supporters. However, in the precinct where a candidate gets weaker support than his/her opponents, oral transmission for him/her is likely to be resisted by his/her opponents' supporters.

② Oral transmission must start in precincts that are connected to precincts where there are many *target voters*. Then, it easily helps to get support. In other words, precincts surrounded by precincts having few *target voters* must not be a starting point of oral transmission.

Criteria for Setting up *Target for Oral Transmission* by Age

① Of the age groups among which a candidate has strong support, the group which is most active in oral transmission becomes the prime target. For example, if a candidate has strong support from twenty- and fifty-year-olds, he/she must establish those in their fifties as the prime target group, because those in their fifties would have more interest in politics and would be more active in oral transmission than those in their twenties.

② If possible, it is better to establish voters in their thirties and forties as the prime target rather than voters in their twenties and fifties, because oral transmission is usually easily delivered from an age group to its adjacent age groups. For example, oral transmission is easily possible from people in their thirties to people in their twenties and forties; oral transmission is easily possible from people in their forties to people in their thirties and fifties. Meanwhile oral transmission is easily possible from those in their twenties only to people in their thirties; oral transmission is easily possible from those above their fifties only to those in their forties.

Criteria for Setting up *Target for Oral Transmission* by Time

① If possible, a candidate makes favorable oral transmission about him/herself to reach voters when most *target voters* decide for whom they will vote.

② In general, oral transmission works more actively in the latter half of a campaign period than earlier, because voters become most interested in the election closer to Election Day. Therefore, it is better for a candidate to spread out oral transmission in favor of him/herself during the latter half of a campaign period.

Criteria for Setting up *Target for Oral Transmission* by Income and Academic Attainment

It is better to start oral transmission in the precincts in which there is little disparity in income and academic attainment among voters, since voters who considerably differ in income and academic attainment do not communicate with one another very much.

(e.2) The Best- and the Worst Oral Transmission

Putting together the criteria described so far, generally each of the best- and worst oral transmissions has the following conditions.

The Best Oral Transmission

① It begins in precincts where a candidate gets the strongest support and is later transferred to precincts where many *target voters* reside.

② Its target by age is those in their thirties and forties.

③ It begins in precincts where there is little disparity in income and academic attainment among voters.

④ It reaches voters when most *target voters* are in the process of deciding for whom they will vote.

The Worst Oral Transmission

① It begins in precincts where a candidate gets the weakest support and is later transferred to precincts where only a few *target voters* reside.

②Its target by age is those in their twenties and those above their fifties.

③ It begins in precincts where there is serious disparity in income and academic attainment among voters.

④ It approaches voters after most *target voters* have decided for whom they will vote, or when most *target voters* are not interested in the election yet.

3. Influence of a Candidate's Characteristics upon Campaigning

Each candidate has his/her own characteristics. These characteristics sometimes hinder candidates to get votes effectively. Below are instances of how a particular characteristic of a candidate can influence his/her campaign.

(1) Candidates who Prefer to Contact only their own Supporters.

These candidates are likely to believe firmly that they win under any circumstances. They are usually career politicians who have been elected several times in a district or are already well known.

Those candidates have no problems in getting votes when their *target voters* are their *fluid supporters*. However, when their *target voters* are their opponents' supporters or undecided voters, they encounter serious problems in obtaining votes from their target.

(2) Candidates who Prefer to Contact only their Opponents' Supporters

These candidates tend to be so ambitious that they believe they can convert their opponents' supporters to support themselves. They are easily found among young candidates or candidates who are running for the first time.

They can get votes effectively, when their *target voters* are their opponents' supporters or undecided voters. However, when their *target voters* are their own supporters, they have a problem in getting votes from their target.

(3) Rational Candidates

Rational candidates are those who make an effort to adapt to the demands of given circumstances. Therefore, they tend to get votes effectively from their *target voters*, regardless of who their target is.

Chapter 5
Candidate Image

1. What is Candidate Image?

Candidate image is the impression of a candidate that voters have in their mind based on incomplete and fragmentary information about a candidate. Voters normally do not have any better source than candidate image for helping them decide on which candidate to support. Therefore, candidate image plays a very important role in getting votes.

Some voters can have a good impression of a candidate by looking at a picture of the candidate that appeared in the media once. For this reason, a candidate always attempts to show him/herself to voters in the best light possible.

For example, when John F. Kennedy ran for senate and later for president, he projected the image of a healthy, strong, and vibrant man who loved sailing and who always had a beautiful suntan, even when the reality was that he was suffering from many different ailments that left him very weak and required several different daily medications.

He was successful in his campaigns, because the public loves to vote for a strong and healthy looking candidate. President Bill Clinton was also aware of the importance of image building. For example, when he was campaigning in 1996, he made sure he was standing among policemen when he spoke about crime. Likewise, when he gave a speech about the environment, he made a point to be at the Grand Canyon or in Rock Creek Park in Washington, D.C.[14]

A candidate's image that voters have could be quite different from what the candidate might really be like. For example, voters might support a candidate, who has gathered much wealth for his/her family, in the hope that, if he/she is elected, he/she will help the economy of the district grow like he/she did for his/her own family. However, it may be easy to see that such candidates do not necessarily make much effort to help the economy of the district grow after they have been elected.

2. Three Characteristics of Candidate Image

① Candidate image is usually not formed in a short period of time. Therefore, it is difficult for a little known candidate, who decides to run a few months before an election, to attain votes with his/her image alone. This is particularly true in a low-profile election to which voters pay little attention.

② Once candidate image is shaped, it is difficult to change it in a short period of time. Therefore, candidates must make an effort to give a good impression of themselves from the beginning.

③ The effectiveness of candidate image is comparative in terms of winning the support of voters. Even if a candidate's image is fine, it may not be effective in getting votes if it is inferior to the opponent's image.

---

[14] Wayne, *The Road to the White House 2000*, 198-199.

3. Four Strategies concerning Candidate Image

(1) Maximized Use of Existing Image

This is used when a candidate's existing image is superior to his/her opponents'. Figure 5.1 shows the case of Candidate Hoichang Lee running for the 1997 presidential election in Korea. Candidate Lee obtained a great reputation of integrity during his public career that led to his becoming a judge of the Supreme Court. Then, during his campaign, he stressed that he was an incorruptible person.

Figure 5.1 Case of Candidate Hoichang Lee who ran for the 1997 presidential election in Korea

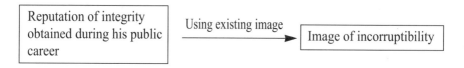

(2) Modification of Existing Image

This is used when a candidate's existing image is insufficient for getting votes effectively. As seen in Figure 5.2, Candidate Daejung Kim tried to transform his radical image that had been formed in the process of his opposition to the dictatorship of military governments, to a softer image in order to get support from the middle class voters who wanted stability in the 1997 presidential election in Korea.

Figure 5.2 Case of Candidate Daejung Kim who ran for the 1997 presidential election in Korea

(3) Importing a Famous Person's Popular Image

This is a strategy of importing the popular image of a famous person to the candidate. This strategy is usually used by a candidate who does not have sufficient time to get voters to recognize him/herself or who does not have a favorable image as the voters would expect.

An example is found in the debate between the Republican vice presidential nominee Dan Quayle and Democratic nominee Lloyd Bentsen in the 1988 presidential election in the United States. During the debate, Candidate Quayle attempted to import a good image of the late president John F. Kennedy by comparing his Senate experience with Kennedy's. However, his attempt to align himself with JFK failed when Candidate Bentsen commented that he knew John F. Kennedy, and added, "You are no John Kennedy."

Another example is seen in Figure 5.3. Candidate Sun Cho, who ran for the 1995 Seoul mayoral election in Korea, attempted to increase voters' recognition of himself rapidly by importing the image of integrity of a popular actor in a television drama series, whose outward appearance was very similar to Sun Cho. This was a very successful attempt, as Sun Cho gained fast recognition.

Figure 5.3 Case of Candidate Sun Cho who ran for the 1995 Seoul mayoral election

Voters' low recognition of Candidate Sun Cho	Importing an actor's popular image ⟶	Rapidly increased voters recognition of Candidate Sun Cho

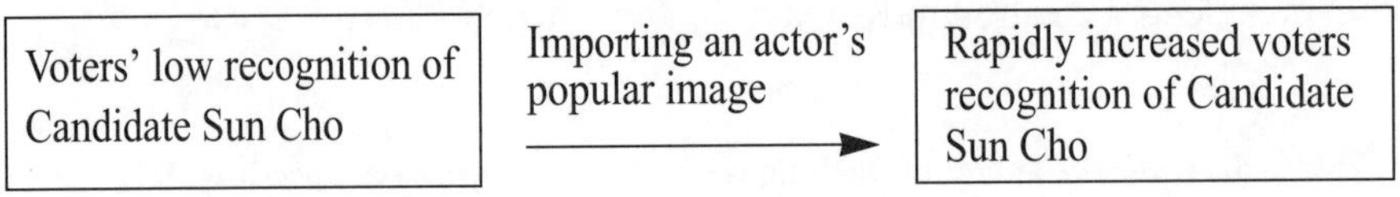

(4) Use of Image Opposite that of a Politician whom Voters Hate

Sometimes, candidates use the image opposite that of an unpopular politician. For example, in the 1980 presidential election in the United States, when Candidate Ronald Reagan ran against the incumbent, Jimmy Carter, who was perceived as a weak leader, Candidate Reagan projected the image of a strong leader by promising a powerful and bullish America. Likewise, as seen in Figure 5.4, in the 1987 presidential election in Korea, Taewoo Noe, one of the main candidates, used this strategy. At that time Doowhan Chun, the incumbent president, was extremely unpopular because of his very authoritative and self-righteous governing style. Then, Candidate Noe consistently stressed that he was democratic unlike President Chun. In fact, at that time voters who were disgusted with the incumbent president's governing style selected Candidate Noe as the next president of Korea.

Figure 5.4 Case of Candidate Taewoo Noe who ran for the 1987 presidential election in Korea

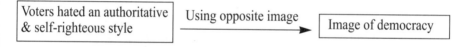

(5) Overlapping Use of Images

Most candidates use more than one image. For example, just before the 1997 presidential election in Korea, Korea's economy was badly depressed, so the incumbent president Youngsam Kim was regarded as incompetent, and people were very unsettled.

As seen in Figure 5.5, Daejung Kim, one of the main candidates, stressed that he was ready to solve the economic problems because he had good knowledge of the economy. He also emphasized that he could stabilize people's restlessness because he was an experienced politician. That is, he simultaneously used both his existing image and the image opposite that of Youngsam Kim.

Figure 5.5 Case of Candidate Daejung Kim who ran for the 1997 presidential election in Korea

| Current incompetent president | Using Opposite image | Candidate who is ready to solve economic problems |
| Restlessness of voters | Using Existing image | Experienced politician who can release voters from restlessness |

4. Strategies for Complementing a Candidate's Deficient Image

Frequently used methods to complement a candidate's deficient image are as follows.

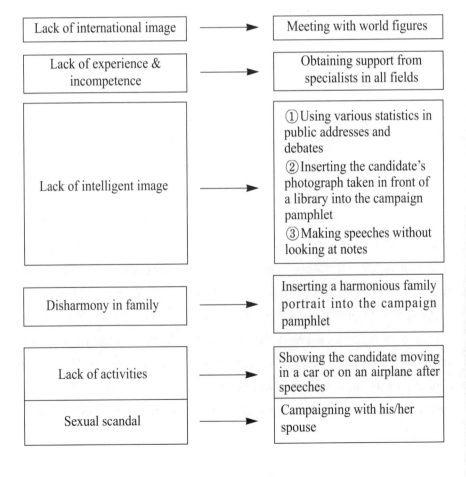

Lack of international image	→	Meeting with world figures
Lack of experience & incompetence	→	Obtaining support from specialists in all fields
Lack of intelligent image	→	① Using various statistics in public addresses and debates ② Inserting the candidate's photograph taken in front of a library into the campaign pamphlet ③ Making speeches without looking at notes
Disharmony in family	→	Inserting a harmonious family portrait into the campaign pamphlet
Lack of activities	→	Showing the candidate moving in a car or on an airplane after speeches
Sexual scandal	→	Campaigning with his/her spouse

5. Images Favored by Voters

As shown in Figure 5.6, older, educated, high-income voters are normally apt to attach importance to candidates' scholarly attainment, career, and policies. Therefore, if they are *target voters*, a candidate should use an image based on the strongest points among his/her scholarly attainments, career, and policies.

Meanwhile, young, poorly educated, low-income voters tend to take a candidate's outward appearance seriously. Therefore, if they are *target voters*, it is better for candidates to project their image related to their outward appearance.

Figure 5.6 Image making based on the kinds of voters

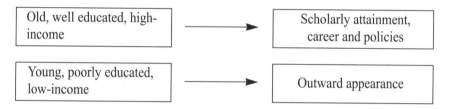

6. Candidate's Image Favored by Voters and Political Circumstances

The following describes the kinds of candidates and candidate images that voters favor under different political environments.

(1) Kinds of Candidates

As seen in Table 5.1, candidates can be divided into experienced and novice. Experienced candidates are ones who have been elected for more than one term. Their strong point is experience in politics, while their weak point is an obsolete way of thinking. Novice candidates are ones who have never been elected. Their strong point is freshness, while their weak point is lack of experience.

Table 5.1 Candidates' strengths and weaknesses

	Experienced	Novice
Strength	Plenty of experience	Freshness
Weakness	Obsolete way of thinking	Lack of experience

(2) Candidate Image Favored by Voters under Different Political Environments

When politics is going well, voters do not need new political figures who can change the current political environment. Therefore, voters prefer experienced candidates to novice candidates. In the meantime, when the political environment is in bad shape, voters prefer novice candidates who can shift the political environment to experienced candidates.

7. Methods for Adopting a Favorable Candidate Image

The following is an example of the process of how a candidate adopts the most favorable image based on the results of a survey.

The first step in projecting a proper image is to find the most desirable image for a candidate. The desirable image for a candidate is certainly different between different levels of elections (presidential, mayoral, etc.). In a presidential election, a candidate is expected to be smart, assertive, and have strong leadership in all countries around the world. In the meantime, in a mayoral election, a candidate is expected to be competent in administering to city affairs.

As seen in Table 5.2, a private survey conducted for a parliamentary election in 1996 in a district in Seoul, Korea showed the respondents' answers to the question, *"What is the most desirable image for parliamentary members?"* *"Trust"* was the answer that 30.4% of the total respondents gave; *"Honesty"*, 17.9%; *"Integrity"*, 15.4%; *"Freshness"*, 15%. *"Experience"* was the answer given by only 10.6% of all respondents. This meant that politics was not going well and voters searched for novice candidates who could change the current political environment.

Table 5.2 Desirable candidate image in the voters' opinion

Trust	Honesty	Integrity	Freshness	Experience	Know-how	Modesty	Good impression
30.4%	17.9%	15.4%	15%	10.6%	6.5%	2.2%	2%

The second step is how voters evaluate each candidate. As seen in Table 5.3, the private survey showed how respondents thought about Candidate Dae C. Jung, who was an incumbent and four-time parliamentary member. Positive responses included *"Experience"* (18.2% of total respondents), *"Good social standing of the candidate's family"* (8.4%), and *"Competence"* (4.4%). Negative responses included *"Not working hard for the district"* (7%).

Table 5.3 Candidate Dae C. Jung's image

Positive image (31%)		Neutral image (41.8%)		Negative image (11.2%)	
Experience	18.2%	Politician	34%	Not working hard for the district	7%
Good family	8.4%	Other	6%	Arrogance	2.8%
Competence	4.4%			Authoritative style	1.4%

＊ Don't know : 16%

As seen in Table 5.4, the private survey showed answers of the respondents to Candidate Sum B. Park's image, who was the opponent of Candidate Jung, a new candidate to this district and a former news anchor of a major television broadcasting station in Korea. Positive answers included *"Trust"* (28.4% of total respondents), *"Honesty"* (5%), and *"Freshness"* (5%). Negative responses reflected only 2.2% of total respondents.

Table 5.4 Candidate Sung B. Park's image

Positive image (30.1%)		Neutral image (39%)		Negative image (2.2%)	
Trust	28.4%	News anchor	33%	Novice politician	0.8%
Honesty	5%	Other	6%	Authoritative style	1.4%
Freshness	5%				
Capability	1.6%				

※ Don't know : 16%

The third step is a comparison of a desirable image in voters' opinion and an image that voters have about each candidate. As shown in Table 5.5, whereas 10.6% of total respondents thought that a parliamentary member must have *"Experience,"* 18.2% thought that Candidate Jung had *"Experience."* In the meantime, while 30.4% of the total respondents thought that a parliamentary member must be *"Trustworthy,"* 28.4% noted that Candidate Park was *"Trustworthy."*

The fourth step is to adopt an image that a candidate stresses in the campaign. Under conditions described so far, it was evident that Candidate Park should stress the image of trust. In contrast, it was not very clear what image Candidate Jung must emphasize. The question was how proper it was for Candidate Jung to stress his experience, when almost all voters wanted the parliamentary member to possess the image of trust, integrity, and freshness. Candidate Jung had to consider ways to damage candidate Park's image of trust rather than emphasizing his own experience to voters.

Table 5.5 Comparison of desirable image to voters and image of Candidates Dae C. Jung and Sung B. Park

	Desirable image	Candidate Jung	Candidate Park
Trust	30.4%		28.4%
Honesty	17.9%		5%
Integrity	15.4%		
Freshness	15%		5%
Experience	10.6%	18.2%	
Know-how	6.5%		
Modesty	2.2%		

8. Projecting an Image that is Similar to the Voters' Experience

A candidate must show to voters that he/she is one of them in every respect in order to get their support. For example, Abraham Lincoln made sure to show voters that he was one of them in the wild frontier. To do this, when campaigning among farmers, he pitched hay, cradled wheat, and split rails.[15]

A candidate must show the following points to voters in order to demonstrate that he/she is one of them.

① He/she understands voters' problems very well. For this, he/she must study voters' problems deeply before contacting them.

② He/she uses the same language as the voters. If the candidate is not familiar with the voters' language, he/she must pay attention to the language the voters use before contacting them.

③ He/she wears the same style of clothes as the voters. A candidate who wears a different style of clothes cannot impress his/her constituents.

---

[15] William Roper, *Winning Politics* (Randor, Pennsylvania: Chilton, 1978) 62.

9. Use of the Image of a Candidate's Spouse

The image of the candidate's spouse is important second to the candidate's, and it can be used for the following purposes.

(1) To Get Votes Independently from the Candidate

This strategy is used when a candidate's spouse has a very fine image. However, it can be used only in the district in which voters permit involvement of a politician's spouse in politics to a degree.

(2) To Complement the Weak Points of the Candidate

This is used when a candidate's spouse has some characteristics that can make up for the candidate's weak points. For example, a candidate's spouse having a soft image can diminish the candidate's rough image. However, we should also be very careful when using this strategy, because if the image of the candidate's spouse is too much better than the candidate's, that could foil the candidate's poor image.

(3) To Reinforce the Strong Points of the Candidate

This is used when a candidate and his/her spouse share strong points. For example, when both a candidate and his/her spouse are experts of the same field, the spouse can help to promote the candidate's image of an expert.

Chapter 6
Themes and Policies in Elections

1. Campaign Theme

(1) What is a Campaign Theme?

A campaign theme determines the direction of a campaign. Candidate image, policies, public promises, or events that take place during the campaign period can also be the subject of the campaign theme. A campaign theme has roughly the following functions.

①A campaign theme transmits a certain message to voters in order to bring out a change in voters' decision. For instance, in the 1988 presidential election, George Bush delivered the message of 'peace and prosperity' to the electorate as a theme. His message meant that if he were to be elected, America would continue to be peaceful and prosperous.[16]

②A campaign theme influences all aspects of a campaign, such as the composition of campaign organization, use of campaign funds, and selection of symbols.

(2) Characteristics of a Campaign Theme

A campaign theme has the following characteristics.

---

[16] Judith Trent and Robert Fridenberg, *Political Campaign Communication* (New York: Praeger, 1991) 227.

(a) Span of Life of the Campaign Theme is Short in an Election to which the Mass Media Pays Close Attention

The span of life of the campaign theme is closely related to how much the election is illuminated by the mass media. Voters are easily bored with themes that are transmitted to voters repeatedly and at high speed. Therefore, the span of life of a campaign theme is short in high-profile elections, such as a presidential election in which the themes of the candidates are delivered to voters by the mass media quickly and repeatedly. In contrast, the span of life of a campaign theme is long in low-profile elections, such as local elections, because the themes must be transmitted by word of mouth rather than the mass media, in which case they spread among the voters rather slowly.

Consequently, candidates running for a presidential election must prepare many themes; those for the local elections need only 2-3 themes.

(b) Too Many Themes cannot Coexist in Elections to which the Mass Media Pays Close Attention.

The mass media can illuminate at best two or three themes at a time. For example, in presidential elections in Korea in which the mass media is the most interested, it is very difficult to get the mass media to become interested in more than three themes at a time. However, in elections in which the mass media is not all that interested, many themes can coexist, because the mass media is not calling the voters' attention to certain themes.

(c) Candidates can Raise Most Themes

Themes can sometimes occur by chance. For example, a serious accident that took place during the campaign period can become the subject of a campaign theme. However, most of the time, it is the candidates themselves who raise the themes.

(3) Kinds of Themes

The kinds of themes can vary. They can be divided into themes for criticism or defense, themes for boosting the candidate's image or stressing policies, and themes for getting support from groups or individuals.

(a) Themes for Criticism or Defense

Themes for criticism are usually employed by candidates who are behind in support and who wish to decrease the support for their opponent(s). For example, a candidate challenging an incumbent candidate, who has increased taxes rapidly, can use "freezing taxes" as his/her campaign theme.

Themes for defense are used by candidates who are ahead of others in support, to keep their support from dropping due to criticism by their opponents.

(b) Themes for Enhancing a Candidate's Image or Stressing Policies

Themes for enhancing a candidate's image are used when voters are very interested in a candidate's image, career, and so on. "Change of generations" is one of the most frequently seen themes for enhancing a candidate's image in Korea. This theme is likely to appeal to voters, who may think that since an incumbent is too old to work enthusiastically, it is better to vote for a young challenger.

Themes for stressing policies are used when most voters are very interested in policies. In many countries, one of the most frequently used themes related to policies is "small government." This theme means reducing interference by government in the lives of citizens in all walks of life.

(c) Themes for Getting Support from Groups or Individuals

Themes for getting support from groups often appear when voters have strong loyalty to groups to which they belong. For example, when almost all voters belong to one of several ethnic groups that are in conflict with one another, a candidate must select a theme to attract voters who belong to the ethnic groups that can help him/her win.

Themes for getting support from individuals are usually employed when most voters are individualistic rather than group-oriented. For instance, when there is a rise in prices due to economic development that happened too fast, "stability" is used as a theme to inform voters that the candidate will freeze the prices if he/she is elected. In the meantime, when the economy is in decline, "change" is often used as a theme to let voters know that the candidate will reform the economic structure in order to get out of an economic slump.

(d) Method to Select Proper Themes

Candidates have to select themes to get votes most effectively. For this, they must know what kinds of voters tend to prefer what kinds of themes.

Table 6.1 shows what kinds of voters are likely to prefer "change" or "stability." "Stability" tends to be preferred by females rather than males, white-collar workers rather than blue-collar workers, old voters rather than young voters, and high-income earners rather than low-income earners. In contrast, "change" is apt to be preferred by males rather than females, blue-collar workers rather than white-collar workers, young voters rather than old voters, and low-income earners rather than high-income earners. For example, it is better for a candidate to choose "change" as his/her campaign theme, when his/her *target voters* are young, blue-collar, or low-income voters.

Table 6.1 Kinds of voters who prefer "stability" or "change"

"Stability"	"Change"
Female, White-collar workers, High-incomer earners, Old voters	Male, Blue-collar workers, Low-income earners, Young voters

Candidates also must know what kinds of candidates are consistent with what kinds of themes. Table 6.2 shows that "stability" tends to be consistent with candidates nominated by the party in power rather than the opposition party, older candidates rather than young candidates, and incumbent candidates rather than challengers. In the meantime, "change" is apt to be consistent with candidates nominated by the opposition party rather than the party in power, young candidates rather than older candidates, and challengers rather than incumbent candidates. For example, it would be better for an older incumbent candidate to select "stability" rather than "change" as his/her campaign theme in order to get votes effectively, if all of his/her other characteristics are very similar to those of his/her opponents.

Table 6.2 Candidates consistent with "stability" or "change"

"Stability"	"Change"
Candidate nominated by the party in power	Candidate nominated by the opposition party
Incumbent candidate	Challenger
Older candidate	Young candidate

Candidates also recognize what kinds of conditions are consistent with "stability" or "change." Table 6.3 shows that when the economy is stable and voters have confidence in politicians, voters are likely to prefer "stability." In this case, it is better for candidates to select "stability" as their campaign theme. In the meantime, when the economy is in a recession, and voters do not have trust in their politicians, the voters are apt to prefer "change." Therefore, under such conditions, it is better for candidates to choose "change" as their campaign theme.

Table 6.3 Conditions that are consistent with "stability" or "change"

"Stability"	"Change"
Booming economy High confidence in politics	Economy in recession Low confidence in politics

(e) Steps to Choose a Proper Campaign Theme

① Carefully analyze all conditions related to the campaign, such as voters' major concerns, degree of economic stability, and *target voters*.

② Select themes that fit the conditions.

③ Campaign based on selected themes.

Figure 6.1 Steps to choose proper campaign themes in the 1997 presidential election in Korea

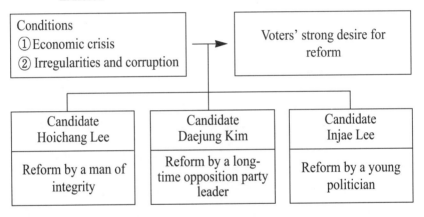

Figure 6.1 shows the steps that each candidate took to choose campaign themes in the 1997 presidential election in Korea.

① Six months before Election Day, there were signs of economic recession all over Korea, and voters observed many irregularities and signs of corruption. Under these circumstances, voters strongly requested that the candidates make radical reforms in the economy and government.

② Thus, all three candidates selected reform as one of their campaign themes. In detail, Candidate Hoichang Lee, who was a candidate of the party in power but was known as very upright, chose "reform by a man of integrity" as his campaign theme; Candidate Daejung Kim, who was the oldest among the three candidates but was a long-time leader of the major opposition party, selected "reform by a long-time opposition party leader" as his campaign theme; Candidate Injae Lee, who was the youngest, picked "reform by a young politician" as his theme.

2. Policies in a Campaign

(1) Importance of Policies

The purpose of an election is to elect capable politicians who effectively plan and implement policies in the interests of the voters. Therefore, policies must be the important factors that are used to get votes in an election.

However, policies do not play such an important role anywhere nowadays for the following reasons. First, many candidates do not keep their public promises once they are elected. Second, overall distrust of politics and politicians also reduces voters' interest in policies. Third, it is not always easy to make voters, most of whom are not interested in politics, to understand the policies of the various candidates. Particularly, it is very difficult to get votes by asserting policies, when there is almost no difference in the policies among the candidates, or when the differences among the policies of the different candidates are only technical.

(2) Kinds of Policies

Classification of policies is important because it helps us understand the candidates' campaign strategies. Policies can be classified as follows.

(a) *Position Policies and Valence Policies*[17]

Position policies refer to policies that clearly divide voters into two groups: supporters for, and dissenters against the candidate. For instance, when a candidate presents a policy promoting public welfare with government funds, low-income families who are expected to get more welfare by paying slightly higher taxes will strongly agree to the policy, while high- and middle-income families who cannot expect more welfare by paying much higher taxes will oppose the policy. *Valence policies* are policies that almost all voters, with rare exception, prefer. Automation of the administrative process, which makes government more efficient than before, is a good example of *valence policies.*

If all other conditions are the same, *position policies* cause more variations of support than *valence policies*. That is, *position policies* that bring about confrontation among the voters stimulate the voters' interest in an election. As a result, they seriously affect the voters' behavior. In contrast, since *valence policies* benefit all voters, it is difficult for them to become hot issues, and it may be difficult for *valence policies* to cause great variations of support among voters.

Therefore, it is desirable for a candidate who is far in advance in support, to present mainly *valence policies* in order to keep the candidate support from changing much. In the meantime, a candidate who falls behind in support must present *position policies* in order to vary the candidate support.

(b) Policies that Affect the Lives of Numerous Voters and Policies that Affect the Lives of only a Handful of Voters

---

[17] *Position policies* and *valence policies* are similar to concepts of "position issue" and "valence issue" each. For concepts of "position issue" and "valence issue," see Angus Campbell, *American Voters* (Chicago: Midway, 1980) 170.

There are policies that affect almost all voters in a district. For instance, policies regarding electronics and water affect almost everyone's economic life. In the meantime, there are policies that would affect only a small number of voters. For example, a policy concerning the redevelopment of a certain area in a district is one that only residents of that area would have any interest in.

If all other conditions are the same, policies that might affect a large number of voters influence the variations in support more than policies that might affect only a small number of voters. Therefore, a candidate leading in support must avoid policies that affect numerous voters, whereas a candidate who is behind others in support must unremittingly present policies that affect many voters.

(c) Policies in which Voters Take Deep Interest and Policies in which Voters have Little Interest

Voters are interested in policies that directly affect their economic and social life. For instance, laborers are naturally deeply concerned with policies about income tax.

On the other hand, voters are not interested in policies that are only indirectly related to their economic and social life. For example, policies concerning providing food to North Korea do not draw considerable attention by the South Koreans, although the mass media usually reports on them extensively.

If all other conditions are the same, policies in which voters are deeply interested influence the variations of support more than policies in which voters have little interest. Therefore, a candidate leading in support must avoid policies about which voters are deeply concerned as much as possible. On the other hand, a candidate who is behind in support must present policies in which voters are deeply interested.

(3) Candidate Support and Policy Presentation

Figure 6.2 shows what is the finest strategy of policy presentation under certain circumstances.

Figure 6.2 Support versus policies

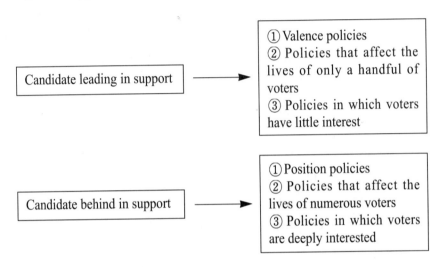

① A candidate who is leading in support has to reduce the variations of support as much as possible. Therefore, he/she must raise *valence policies*, policies in which only a handful of voters are interested, as well as policies in which voters are not deeply interested.

② A candidate who is behind in support must amplify the variations of support. Therefore, he/she must raise *position policies*, policies in which a large number of voters are interested, as well as policies in which voters are deeply interested.

(4) Strategies of Policy Presentation when *Target voters* are Set up

The following strategies are suggested, when *target voters* are already set up.

① When a candidate's weak supporters are his/her *target voters*, the candidate has to defend them from attack of his/her opponents. Therefore, he/she must present *valence policies* with which all of his/her weak supporters agree.

② When a candidate's target is undecided voters, the candidate must present policies that a majority of undecided voters favor.

③ When a candidate's *target voters* are his/her opponent's weak supporters, the candidate must present *position policies* to break up the target.

Chapter 7
The Campaign Organization

1. The Importance of the Campaign Organization

The campaign organization, which is a center for making and implementing campaign strategies, plays an important role in campaigns and considerably affects the election results. However, it is difficult to acknowledge its importance, because only its members know what is going on in it and they are the only ones who are in a position to evaluate the organization's activities.

The following is somewhat partial,[18] but still meaningful evidence to prove the influence of a campaign's organization on how an election turns out. Table 7.1 shows part of the results of in-depth interviews conducted with 60 key organization members working for Candidate Dae C. Jung, who ran for a district in Seoul right after the 1996 parliamentary election in Korea. Those organization members included the campaign manager, precinct chairmen, and coffee coordinators, who were all directly involved in the campaign activities.

The first interview question was, *"What is the most important factor that affected the election results?"* Factors related to the efficiency of the

---

[18] Interviews were conducted by the author from June to August in 1996.

campaign organization, such as properness of campaign strategies, capacity of organization in implementing campaign strategies, and level of cooperation among members, were among the factors that 71.6% of the respondents mentioned as the most important in gaining votes. In the meantime, only 18.4% thought that factors beyond the campaign organization, such as campaigning by the central party organization and unexpected accidents taking place during the campaign period, were important in gaining votes. Both factors related to the efficiency of the campaign organization and factors beyond the organization were considered important according to 5% of the respondents, while another 5% said *"Don't know."*

Table 7.1 Factors influencing election results

Factors related to the efficiency of the campaign organization	Factors beyond the campaign organization	Both	Don't know
71.6%	18.4%	5%	5%

It is difficult to generalize the survey results above, since they are based on interviews with the campaign organization members of only one candidate. However, these results should not be ignored because they reflect the answers of people who were at the scene of the campaign.

2. Factors Impeding the Effectiveness of the Campaign Organization

Most campaigns are not very well organized because they have imminent chronic problems. These problems can be divided into (a) disharmony among the organization members, including the staff members and canvassers, and (b) discord between the candidate and organization members.

(a) Disharmony among the Organization Members

Effectiveness of the campaign organization relies on how well its members cooperate with one another. There exist several factors impeding harmonious cooperation among campaign organization members, which include the following.

Complexity of the Organization

Discord occurring in a simple organization composed of 3-5 persons tends to be easily resolved because the number of people related to the discord is very small and they are working closely. However, discord in a complex organization composed of nearly 100 people may not be resolved easily because too many people are involved in the discord.

Most campaign organizations are complex. Campaign organizations for a presidential election and for the mayoral election of a big city are usually composed of several hundred people. Even campaign organizations for elections for congressional members and small city mayors are made up of more than 50 people, including core staff members and persons in charge of each precinct. Therefore, discord in the campaign organization cannot be resolved easily.

Lack of a Commanding System in the Campaign Organization

Effectiveness is low in an organization in which high-ranking organization members do not have the carrot and the stick to make the low-ranking members follow their orders. The campaign organization is one such organization. In detail, the campaign organization is only a temporary workplace for most of the members, because most organization members go to other jobs after the election, regardless of the results of the election. Therefore, low-ranking members have no reason except moralistic reasons to follow the high-ranking members' orders well, so that it is very difficult to sustain a chain of command in the organization. In reality, we can easily see that organization members neglect to perform or even resist the high-ranking members' orders in the campaign organization.

The Crucial Role of Low Rankers

In low-profile elections, low rankers play a more important role than high rankers do in getting votes. Candidates running for low-profile elections must rely on personal, telephone and mail contacts with voters conducted by low rankers, who are usually long-time residents in the district, for getting votes. However, there usually are very few long-time residents willing to serve as low rankers to go around, and if they leave the organization, it is almost impossible for the candidate to replace them with persons who can offer comparable quality of service. This condition allows the low rankers to refuse or to idly carry out the orders of high rankers.

This problem is usually less serious in high-profile elections such as presidential and senatorial elections, in which the mass media, controlled by high rankers, plays an important role. Consequently, in high-profile elections, high rankers have more power to control low rankers.

Absence of the Candidate's Commanding Power

Most candidates clearly recognize discord and lack of commanding system within the campaign organization. However, they cannot resolve this problem for the following two reasons.

First, candidates physically and mentally feel tired and also do not have enough time to take care of their organizations because of their busy campaign schedule. Second, candidates need as many helpers as they can. Under this condition, if the candidate takes sides with one of the factions in discord, the other faction is likely to break away from the organization and, in the worst case scenario, even join the opponent's organization.

(b) Discord between a Candidate and Organization Members

Discord between a candidate and organization members is also one of the factors that can impede the effectiveness of the campaign organization. This discord is usually caused by the following three factors.

The Candidate's Distrust of the Capacity of Organization Members

In order for the campaign to be effective, the candidate must relegate appropriate responsibility to each organization member and he/she must be open to suggestions from the members. However, it frequently happens that the candidate cannot tolerate the directions that the campaign staffers might suggest to him/her. As a result, the staffers may lose interest and motivation in supporting the candidate, and they may work rather passively, doing no more than what the candidate asks them to do.

Recruiting New Organization Members

The candidate recruits new members into the campaign organization, since he/she believes that the existing members, who have worked for the organization for a long time before the campaign period, are incompetent.

Then, the candidate tends to accept the new members' suggestions rather than those of the existing members. This in turn may cause the existing members to feel antagonistic against the candidate and may result in discord between new and existing members. Confrontation can reach an extreme, particularly if there is a high chance that the newly recruited members will remain in the organization after the election. This can throw the campaign organization into confusion.

The Organization Members' Insufficient Experience and Knowledge about the Campaign

Most organization members do not have much knowledge and experience in the campaign. Although some organization members have experience, it can hardly help the current campaign, as their experience is usually obtained from the election of two years ago. This lack of experience and knowledge usually damages the effectiveness of the campaign. Its visible negative result is that even though an effective and scientific campaign plan is made, the organization members cannot execute the plan, because they cannot understand it very well.

3. Ineffectiveness of Campaign Organizations

Most campaign organizations are very ineffective. It is very difficult to find organizations that can steadily implement the planned strategy and adapt to the revised plan caused by unexpected accidents that take place during the campaign period.

Let us return to the survey above. For the question, *"How effective is the campaign organization?"* 57 out of 60 members responded that the organization was very ineffective. All 31 key staff members, including the campaign manager, the head of the planning team, and the organization manager, answered so. According to the author's observations, these answers certainly are true in almost all campaign organizations at all levels of elections in Korea.

In the interviews, the participants were asked to give reasons for the ineffectiveness of a campaign organization, as shown in Table 7.2. Of the

Table 7.2 Reasons why the campaign organization is ineffective

Rank	Reason	Percentage
1	Indifference of the organization members caused by discord among the members	45%
2	Lack of campaign funds and canvassers	30%
3	Lack of responsibility and negligence of organization members	6.6%
4	Other	18.4%

total respondents, 45% answered, the indifference of the organization members caused by discord among them; 30% replied, lack of campaign funds and canvassers; 6.6% said, irresponsibility and negligence of the organization members.

According to the author's observations, the campaign organization members' insufficient experience in campaigning and their lack of understanding of campaign strategies may have also impeded the effectiveness of the organization. However, the organization members who were interviewed did not agree with this conclusion.

4. Effective and Ineffective Campaign Organizations

The effectiveness of a campaign organization originates from various factors. However, the level of harmonious cooperation between the strategy planning team and the strategy implementing team has been the most important factor that determines the degree of the effectiveness of a campaign organization in almost all cases in Korea. The following is about how the relationship between the two teams affects the effectiveness of a campaign organization.

(1) The most Ineffective Campaign Organization

As shown in Figure 7.1, in an ineffective campaign organization, the strategy planning team and the implementing team never cooperate with each other, while both teams communicate with only the candidate. In this organization, the candidate has to transmit the campaign plan made by the planning team to the implementing team. This kind of campaign organization usually has the following characteristics.

① Since the candidate must play a role as a messenger between the two teams, he/she cannot pay attention to the campaign as much as he/she must.

② The candidate remains in the campaign office for only a few hours because of other campaign activities. Therefore, the plan made by the planning team cannot be conveyed to the implementing team at the right time.

Figure 7.1 The most ineffective campaign organization

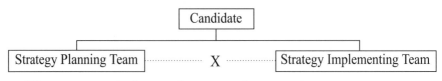

※ 'X' means cooperation between the two teams is not smooth.

The phenomenon above usually takes place for the following reasons. The candidate thinks that the existing organization members, who have been working for the candidate since before the campaign period, are not capable of devising an appropriate strategy plan; thus, he/she recruits new members to devise campaign strategies. The newcomers also think that since the existing members are not capable of planning the strategies, they should implement the plan under the new members' directions. Meanwhile, the existing staff members do not admit the newcomers' ability, because they think that the newcomers do not have enough experience in the district.

As a rule, the old team, assigned to implement the new team's plans, does not sincerely carry out the plan transmitted to it through the candidate because of confrontation between the old and new teams. This style of organization loses a considerable part of its energy, and therefore cannot be effective in obtaining votes.

(2) A Campaign Organization that is Average in Effectiveness

This is an organization in which cooperation between the planning team and the implementing team is inharmonious, but a campaign director who is able to control them can command both sides.

Figure 7.2 A campaign organization that is average in effectiveness

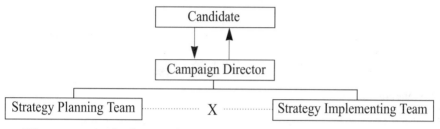

※ 'X' means cooperation between the two teams is not smooth.

This kind of campaign organization has the following characteristics.

① The candidate can devote his/her time and energy to the campaign activities, because he/she does not need to take care of controlling the organization.

② The campaign strategies can be implemented as planned to some degree, because the campaign director, who remains in the campaign office most of time, enforces the implementing team to carry out the strategies devised by the planning team.

(3) The most Effective Campaign Organization

As seen in Figure 7.3, this is an organization in which the campaign director, who remains in the campaign office and also has strong power over the organization, controls the organization. At the same time, there is also smooth and direct cooperation between the strategy planning team and the strategy implementing team.

Figure 7.3 The most effective campaign organization

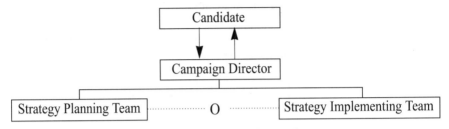

※ 'O' means cooperation between the two teams is smooth.

This kind of organization usually has the following strong points.

① The candidate can devote his/her time and energy to campaign activities, because he/she does not need to take care of controlling the organization.

② The campaign director uses his/her time and energy for matters besides controlling the organization, because direct cooperation between the planning team and the implementing team is running smoothly without his/her intervention.

③ Direct and smooth communication between the planning team and the implementing team maximizes the effectiveness of the campaign. The implementing team can carry out strategies well, because the planning team directly conveys its plan to the implementing team with detailed explanations. On the other hand, the implementing team lets the planning team know what takes place on the scene and helps it to adjust its strategies daily, so that the strategies stay on target.

5. Real Example of an Ineffective Campaign Organization

Figure 7.4 is a real example of the campaign organization of Candidate

Myung C. Lee who ran for the 1996 parliamentary election in a district in Seoul. This formal campaign organization chart shows that the campaign director controls both the strategy planning team and the implementing team under the supervision of the campaign chairman. However, this chart was not followed in operating the organization, for the reasons given below.

① An eminent person residing in the district was designated as the campaign chairman, but he was not endowed with authority to lead the organization; nor did he have the ability to control the organization.

② The campaign director joined the organization just one month before the election, while both heads of the planning team and the implementing team had worked long before the election. Then the heads of both the planning team and the implementing team did not admit the authority of the campaign director.

③ There was also severe conflict between the heads of the planning team and the implementing team. The head of the planning team thought that the

Figure 7.4 Formal structures of the organization

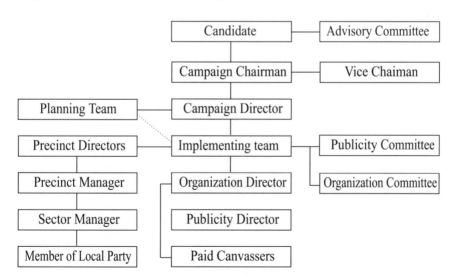

head of the implementing team only knew old-fashioned campaign methods, while the head of the implementing team thought that the head of the planning team did not have enough experience in the district.

④ Many people were assigned as members of advisory organs, such as vice chairman, advisory committee to the Candidate Lee, publicity committee, and organization committee. However, their positions were just nominal.

Figure 7.5 shows how this organization operated in reality. Candidate Lee had to transmit the strategy devised by the planning team to the implementing team for the following two reasons. First, the campaign director who was alienated from both heads of the strategy planning team and the strategy implementing team could not play an effective role in transmitting the strategy to the implementing team. Second, the implementing team did not cooperate with the planning team at all.

Figure 7.5 Organization structure that was actually operated

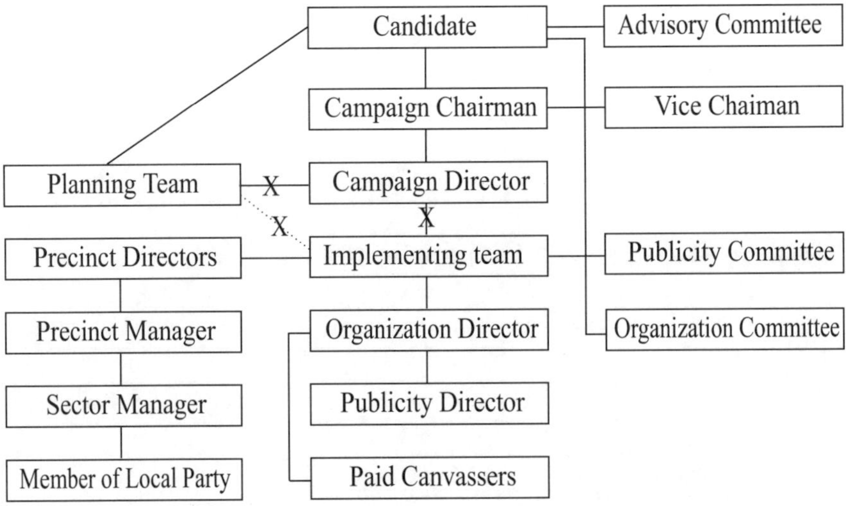

* 'X' means cooperation between organs or direction of high rank over low rank is not smooth.

Furthermore, as Election Day approached, Candidate Lee became too busy to serve as a messenger between the two teams. Consequently, the strategy devised by the planning team was not delivered to the implementing team and became useless; meanwhile, the implementing team made its own crude strategy and executed it. This resulted in a very ineffective campaign, even if Candidate Lee still won the election.

6. Suggestions for Establishing an Effective Campaign Organization

Following are some suggestions to resolve the kinds of problems of a campaign organization described above.

① The candidate must appoint a campaign director who has knowledge and experience of public relations, campaign strategies, and surveys and he/she must empower that director to control the organization.

② The candidate must serve as a model who follows the advice of the aids.

③ The candidate should resist the temptation to employ new members as far as he/she can. If possible, it is better for the candidate to hire a campaign expert rather than employing new members. The campaign expert does not provoke the existing members' resistance because he/she is certain to leave the organization after the election and because he/she knows the characteristics of a campaign organization and its members, and therefore can work well with the existing members.

④ If the candidate must employ new members, he/she must select people who can work harmoniously with the existing members. It is also desirable to hire persons who evidently will leave the organization after the election. If possible, new members must be placed in a lower rank than the existing members, because otherwise the existing members would have antagonistic feelings toward the newcomers.

7. Canvass Organization

Getting votes is only one important purpose of the political campaign, carried out by candidates and canvassers. However, not every canvasser can obtain votes by asking voters to support the candidate whom he/she is promoting. Some unqualified canvassers can in fact cause the candidate to lose votes. Therefore, each canvasser must be evaluated in terms of his/her quality and ability and he/she must be assigned appropriate roles before sending him/her out into the field.

(1) Campaign Activities

As shown in Figure 7.6, campaign activities include the following: *asking for support, positive oral transmission, negative oral transmission, and demonstrating the strength of support for the candidate.*

Figure 7.6 Campaign activities

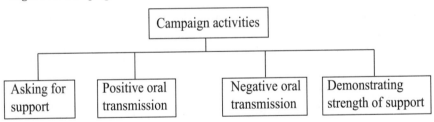

① *Asking for support* is an activity in which canvassers directly ask voters to support the candidate whom they are promoting.

② *Positive oral transmission* is an activity in which canvassers talk to voters about the positive characteristics of the candidate they are promoting. Its purpose is to give voters a friendly feeling toward the candidate so that they will vote for him/her.

③ *Negative oral transmission* is an activity in which canvassers talk to voters about the negative characteristics of the opponents. Its aim is to give the voters an unfavorable feeling toward the opponents so that they will not vote for the opponents.

④ *Demonstrating the strength of support for the candidate* is an activity, such as a rally or a march, showing that a large number of canvassers are working for the candidate.

(2) Kinds of Canvassers

Canvassers can be divided into four kinds: *support seekers, positive oral transmitters, negative oral transmitters,* and *canvassers who hold demonstrations for the candidate.* Table 7.3 shows the campaign activities that each kind of canvasser can undertake.

Table 7.3 Campaign activities that each kind of canvasser can effectively undertake

	Asking for support	Positive oral transmission	Negative oral transmission	Demonstrating strength of support
Support seekers	X	X	X	X
Positive oral transmitters		X	X	X
Negative oral transmitters			X	X
Canvassers who hold demonstrations for the candidate				X

(a) *Support Seekers*

These are canvassers who can obtain a vote by directly asking for support from voters without giving them a negative impression of the candidate. They include the candidate's family and leading figures in the district. The candidate's family members are *support seekers* because they are closely concerned about his/her success. Leading figures in the district are naturally *support seekers* because most voters respect them.

Support seekers can also do *positive oral transmission* for the candidate, *negative oral transmission* against the opponents, and can also participate in demonstrations for the candidate.

(b) *Positive Oral Transmitters*

These are canvassers who can spread positive information about the candidate to voters around them. They are usually small business owners and shopkeepers who talk to a lot of customers every day. Voters usually do not respect them but may trust them to some degree, because they are known to have a lot of interactions with different people every day, and they would have a lot of information about the elections.

Therefore, it is good for them to give positive impressions about the candidate or tell a positive anecdote about him/her, because voters would believe them. However, it would be better if they did not ask directly for the voters' support, since this may call forth an antagonistic reaction against the candidate. *Positive oral transmitters* can also do *negative oral transmission* against opponents, and participate in demonstrations for a candidate.

(c) *Negative Oral Transmitters*

These are canvassers who cannot be trusted because they are usually unemployed persons whom the candidate has hired to speak for him/her. They attend rallies or community meetings, where they spread negative publicity about the opponents among the crowd. Voters usually react negatively to such oral transmitters when they *ask for support* or do *positive oral transmission* for a candidate, because voters have no confidence in their loyalty and cannot trust their word.

Therefore, it is better to use them for only *negative oral transmission* against the opponents, since voters tend to believe *negative oral transmission*, regardless of who spreads it. *Negative oral transmitters* can also participate in demonstrations for a candidate.

(d) *Canvassers who Hold Demonstrations for a Candidate*

These are canvassers who do not necessarily reside in the district, but are temporarily hired to hold demonstrations. They know only a few voters in the district and therefore cannot do even *negative oral transmission* against opponents, and can only participate in a demonstration, such as a rally or a march.

(3) Proper Use of Canvassers under Various Circumstances

Table 7.4 shows a hypothetical example of what kinds of canvassers are needed for which candidates. As indicated in Table 7.4, three candidates are in competition and they have different degrees of voters' recognition of, and support for themselves. As seen in Table 7.4, voters' name recognition of Candidate A is as high as 90%, which is the maximum that candidates can usually get in an election.

Therefore, it is hardly expected that support for Candidate A would increase much with an increase in voters' recognition of him/herself. Consequently, Candidate A must stress suppressing the rise of support for Candidate B and Candidate C by using mainly *negative oral transmitters* from the beginning to the end of the campaign and executing a negative campaign against them.

As seen in Table 7.4, voters' recognition of Candidate B is only 60%, which can rise to 90%. Therefore, Candidate B should make an effort to raise voters' recognition of him/herself. At the same time, he/she must do negative campaigning to reduce support for Candidate A and to suppress the rapid increase in support for Candidate C.

Therefore, at the early stages of the campaign, Candidate B must use *support seekers* and *positive oral transmitters* to get votes and use *negative oral transmitters* to reduce support for Candidate A and suppress the abrupt increase in support for Candidate C. When voters' recognition of Candidate B

Table 7.4 Proper uses of canvassers under various circumstances

Candidate	Voters' recognition of candidate	Support for candidate	Degree of rise of support	Proper canvassers
A	90%	30%	Small increase in support	Early stages of the campaign: Negative oral transmitters Latter stage of the campaign: Negative oral transmitters
B	60%	20%	Average increase in support	Early stages of the campaign: Support seekers, Positive & Negative oral transmitters Latter stage of the campaign: Negative oral transmitters
C	30%	10%	Radical increase in support	Early stages of the campaign: Support seekers & Positive oral transmitters Latter stage of the campaign:Negative oral transmitters

rises to 90%, he/she must focus on only reducing support for Candidate A and suppressing the rise of support for Candidate C by using mainly *negative oral transmitters*.

As indicated in Table 7.4, voters' recognition of Candidate C is at best 30%. Accordingly, it is anticipated that the rise of voters' recognition of him/her comes with rapid increase of support. Therefore, he/she must get votes with a canvassing organization made up of mainly *support seekers* and *positive oral transmitters* in the early stages of the campaign. When voters' recognition of the candidate rises to 90%, he/she must stress reducing support for Candidate A and Candidate B by using *negative oral transmitters* and executing a negative campaign against them.

8. Conditions Necessary for Canvassers to Implement a Successful Campaign

Figure 7.7 shows four conditions that are necessary for canvassers' successful implementation of planned strategies.

Figure 7.7 Conditions for canvassers to implement successful campaign

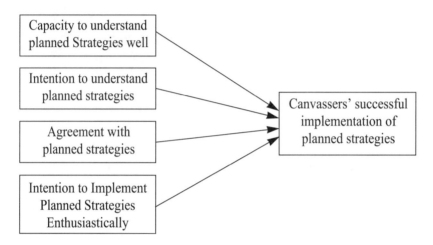

(1) Capacity to Understand Planned Strategies Well

Campaign strategies are not so simple, and canvassers usually have a difficult time understanding them. Therefore, canvassers must be thoroughly instructed before they implement a campaign strategy.

(2) Intention to Understand Planned Strategies

Some canvassers do not even attempt to understand campaign strategies, because canvassing is only a minor matter to them. Candidates must therefore be sure to check that their canvassers understand the campaign strategy well.

(3) Agreement with Planned Strategies

Many canvassers have their own ideas about how to canvass, which are often quite different than the planned strategies. In this case, members of the implementing team must give enough explanations and appropriate data to persuade the canvassers to follow the planned strategies.

(4) Intention to Implement Planned Strategies Enthusiastically

Canvassing is not the most important thing to many canvassers; they canvass only when they have spare time. To solve this problem, some of the organization members must work to encourage and supervise canvassers' activities.

Chapter 8
Methods for Effectively Distributing Resources

It is very difficult to find candidates who have enough resources to use in order to run a successful campaign. There are two reasons for this. First, almost none of the candidates have human and material resources as much as they would like. Second, the electoral law has put some restraints on the resources that candidates can use. Consequently, they must learn to strategize in order to distribute insufficient resources available to them most effectively during the campaign period so that they can get the maximum number of votes.

Resources for a campaign include both material and human resources. Funding is core of material resources because it helps candidates to buy paid advertising and enables other campaign activities such as the bus tour around the district. Human resources include core staff members, professional campaign consultants, paid canvassers, and volunteers. Some of them can be bought with funds; others, such as volunteers, may be obtained through the candidate's good image or personal relationships.

In this chapter, the campaign period is divided into the early stages, the middle stages, and the last stage in order to explain the methods for effectively distributing resources. For instance, assuming a candidate begins to campaign within three months prior to an election, the early stages would be the period between three months to two months before the election, the middle stages would be the period between two months to one month before the election, and the last stage would be the period from one month before the election to the day of the election. In most elections, while candidates tend to use resources to raise the level of voters' recognition of them in the early stages of the campaign, they are apt to use up their remaining resources in order to differentiate themselves from their opponents during the middle and last stages.

1. Methods to Distribute Resources to Specific Precincts

A candidate running for office needs to find how much of the resources must be distributed to specific precincts in his/her district to get votes effectively. In this chapter, under the assumption that *target voters* are already detected, factors that are taken into account in order to effectively distribute resources to precincts are described, as seen in Figure 8.1.

(1) Number of *Target Voters* in Precincts

Before deciding how much of the resources are allocated to each precinct, we must know the number of *target voters* in each precinct. Provided all other conditions are very similar among the precincts, the more *target voters* a precinct has, the more resources that have to be allocated to it.

If the voting rates and density of *target voters* are quite different from one precinct to another, they are also considered in addition to the number of *target voters* in each precinct. If the number of *target voters* is quite similar among the precincts, more resources should be allocated to precincts where the voting rates and density of *target voters* are higher.

Figure 8.1 Criteria for effectively distributing resources

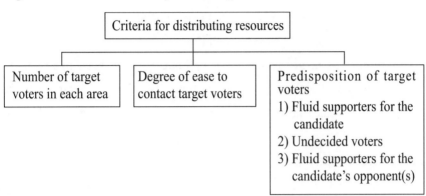

(2) Degree of Ease to Contact *Target Voters*

More resources are needed in the precincts where it is more difficult to contact *target voters*, because the harder it is to contact the *target voters*, the more frequent attempts to contact them are necessary to get their support.

(3) Supporting Predisposition of *Target Voters*

When *target voters* are leaning in favor of voting for a candidate's opponents, the candidate needs the largest amount of resources, in order to persuade his/her *target voters* to change their minds. In the meantime, when a candidate's *target voters* are favorable to him/her, the least amount of resources is needed, because the only work the candidate has to do is to keep those continued support of *target voters*. When *target voters* are undecided voters, necessary resources fall somewhere between the middle of these two cases.

※ Hypothetical Example of Distributing Resources to Specific Precincts

The district where Candidate P is running is divided into three target precincts, A, B and C. These precincts have very similar voting rates and density of *target voters*. The following describes the simplest method to distribute resources effectively among the precincts.

(1) Number of *Target Voters* in each Precinct

The number of *target voters* for Candidate P is the least in Precinct A, twice as many in Precinct B, and three times as many in Precinct C. Then, Candidate P assigns 1 point to Precinct A, 2 points to Precinct B, and 3 points to Precinct C.

(2) Degree of Ease in Contacting *Target Voters*

In degree of ease in contacting *target voters*, Precinct A comes first, Precinct B comes second, and Precinct C comes third. Therefore, Candidate P assigns 1 point to Precinct A, 2 points to Precinct B, and 3 points to Precinct C.

(3) Voters' Supporting Predisposition

A campaign is more effective in the precincts where there are a large number of voters who are favorable to the candidate than the precincts where only a few voters are favorable to the candidate. The reason is that a candidate's campaign is assisted by his/her supporters' oral transmission in the precincts where there are a large number of voters favorable to the candidate.

From the perspective of voters' supporting predisposition, Precinct A has the largest number of voters who are favorable to Candidate P among the three precincts, so it is the easiest for Candidate P to campaign in Precinct A. Since Precinct B is in the middle in the number of voters favorable to Candidate P, it is also in the middle in the degree of ease in campaigning for Candidate P in Precinct B. Precinct C has the largest number of voters favorable to Candidate P's opponent, so that it is the hardest for Candidate P to campaign in Precinct C. Thus, Candidate P assigns 1 point to Precinct A, 2 points to Precinct B, and 3 points to Precinct C.

Table 8.1 shows the subtotal of the points of each precinct with the points of the three variables mentioned above. It also shows the ratio of the subtotal points of each precinct out of the total points combining the points of each precinct. The rates are 1/6th in Precinct A, 1/3rd in Precinct B and 1/2 in Precinct C. This means that it is desirable for Candidate P to distribute 1/6th of the resources available to him to Precinct A, 1/3rd to Precinct B, and 1/2 to Precinct C.

Table 8.1 Hypothetical example of distributing resources to precincts

Precinct	Number of target voters	Degree of ease in contacting target voters	Voters' predisposition	Subtotal
A	1 point	1 point	1 point	3 point(1/6)
B	2 point	2 point	2 point	6 point(1/3)
C	3 point	3 point	3 point	9 point(1/2)

2. Proper Point of Time to Use Resources

When must a candidate use resources to obtain the maximum number of votes? This depends on who the candidate's *target voters* are.

(1) When a Candidate's *Target Voters* are his/her *Fluid Supporters*

When a candidate's *target voters* are his/her *fluid supporters*, he/she has to use resources as early as possible to promptly transform his/her *target voters* into *fixed supporters* for the following reasons.

① It is more difficult for the opponent to effectively attack a candidate's *fixed supporters* than it is to attack his/her *fluid supporters*.

② A candidate's *fixed supporters* do more frequent and strong oral transmission for the candidate than do his/her *fluid supporters*.

(2) When a Candidate's *Target Voters* are Undecided Voters

When a candidate's *target voters* are undecided voters, he/she has to spend most of his or her resources during the period that *target voters* decide for whom they will vote.

(a) When Target Voters Decide in the Early Stages of a Campaign Period

Target voters usually decide for whom they will vote in the early stages of a campaign period, when they have great interest in the election but they do not have enough information about the candidates. In this case, the candidates must spend most of their resources in the early stages of a campaign period, in order to provide maximum information about them to voters. In general, old, high-income, or well-educated voters are likely to make a decision in the early stages of a campaign period.

(b) When *Target Voters* Decide in the Last Stage of a Campaign Period

Target voters usually decide for whom they will vote in the last stage of a campaign period, when they have little interest in the election. These voters begin to think about whom they will support, only when they are forced to go to the polling booth to fulfill their duty. In this case, a candidate must spend most of his or her resources in the last stage of the campaign period. Young, low-income, or poorly educated voters tend to make a decision in the last stage of a campaign period.

(3) When a Candidate's *Target Voters* are his/her Opponent's *Fluid Supporters*

Getting support from the opponent's *fluid supporters* requires a long time and a lot of resources. When a candidate's *target voters* are mainly his/her opponent's *fluid supporters*, he/she must continue to put more resources than his/her opponent from the beginning to the end of the campaign period.

3. Methods to Distribute Resources Depending on the Level of Voters' Recognition of Candidates

(1) Candidates Little Recognized by Voters

As seen in Figure 8.2, candidates little recognized by voters must spend most of their resources in the early stages of the campaign period to raise voters' recognition of them as quickly as possible. The increase in support due to increased voters' recognition is usually connected to the growing number of volunteers and funds donated to them. With increased human and material resources, candidates must get more votes in the middle and last stages of the campaign period.

In a presidential election, a candidate usually spends a large amount of resources early in the campaign to attract the media, which is an important channel to help him/her get recognized. Once voters' recognition of the candidate is established and he/she becomes one of the main competitors, the candidate can easily expand his/her organization into many more states beyond the central organization in the capital.

Figure 8.2 Method of effective distribution of resources for little recognized candidates

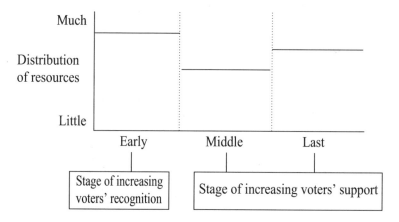

(2) A Highly Recognized Candidate Competing with Little Recognized Opponent(s)

As Figure 8.3 shows, a highly recognized candidate in competition with little recognized opponents is better off spending most of his or her resources in the middle and last stages of the campaign period. This is because spending most of the resources in the early stages of the campaign period heats the election, which in turn increases voters' interest in the election and helps little recognized opponents raise the voters' recognition of them.

If little recognized candidates fail to increase voters' recognition of them in spite of the fact that they spent most of their resources in the early stages of the campaign period, a highly recognized candidate competing with them does not necessarily spend his/her resources in the middle and last stages.

Figure 8.3 Method of effective distribution of resources for a highly recognized candidate competing with little recognized opponent(s)

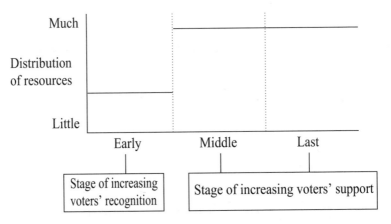

(3) A Highly Recognized Candidate Competing with Highly Recognized Opponent(s)

In the competition among highly recognized candidates, while the period for increasing voters' recognition of them is omitted, the period for getting support opens during the early stages of the campaign period. In this case, the method for effectively distributing resources depends on when *target voters* make a decision on whom to support.

When *target voters* answer in the survey that they tend to decide whom they will support in the early stages of the campaign period, a candidate should accordingly spend most of his/her resources early in the campaign.

The candidate who is far ahead of others by successfully getting votes in the early stages of the campaign may enjoy the *bandwagon effect*, the instinct of voters to prefer to be on the winning side. That is, the front-runner may obtain support from voters without serious campaigning for their votes.

Meanwhile, when *target voters* answer in the survey that they tend to decide whom they will support in the last stage of the campaign period, a candidate should use most of his/her resources later in the campaign in order to secure support of *target voters*.

4. Another Method for Effectively Distributing Resources

Votes can be effectively obtained if a candidate spends his/her resources around the time of a big event related to the campaign.[19] For example, a candidate can focus his/her paid media advertising around a television debate among the candidates. The principle of this strategy is that a candidate can win votes most effectively if he/she spends his/her resources for the campaign when voters are most interested in the election.

---

[19] This method is called "the really big show strategy" in Trent and Fridenberg, *Political Campaign Communication*, 287.

Chapter 9
Types of Campaigns and their Effectiveness

Campaigns can be divided into two kinds: a campaign in which candidates and canvassers contact voters to ask for their support; and a campaign that depends on oral transmission among voters about the candidates and the election. In this chapter, the effectiveness of two methods is evaluated.

1. Candidates and Canvassers' Contact with Voters

(1) Kinds of Contacts

Candidates and canvassers can use two types of contacts with voters: the direct and indirect channels. The direct channel is a method in which candidates and canvassers ask voters face-to-face to support the candidate. It includes two ways.

① Face-to-face contact with voters

② Public address in front of voters

The indirect channel is a method in which candidates contact voters through a medium, such as the following:

① The mass media like television, radio, and newspapers

② Public booklets and pamphlets

③ Telephone or mail

Since the number of voters in high-profile elections, such as presidential and governor elections, is at least more than one million, candidates and canvassers can only contact at best 1% of the total voters face-to-face during the campaign period.

Therefore, only the indirect channel method, such as television debates and newspaper advertisements, greatly affects election results, while the direct channel method does not play an important role in these elections. In the meantime, both direct and indirect methods are crucial for low-profile elections in which the number of voters is small and thus the candidates and canvassers can contact a considerable number of voters face-to-face.

(2) Evaluation of the Effectiveness of each Campaign Method

There are two criteria for evaluating the effectiveness of each campaign method. The first is how many voters can be contacted through each method. The second is how positive the response from voters contacted through each method can be.

(a) How Many Voters can be Contacted through each Method

A campaign method cannot be regarded as very effective if only a very small number of the total voters can be contacted through that method. Table 9.1 shows how many voters can be contacted through each campaign method.

Table 9.1 Number of voters contacted through each campaign method

Campaign method	Number of contacted voters
Candidate's public address	Few
Candidate's face-to-face contact with voters	Few
Candidate's contact with voters through the mass media	Great many
Canvassers' contact with voters face-to-face or by phone	Many

There are two reasons why a *candidate's public address* is not very effective in contacting many voters. First, it is physically impossible for a candidate to make more than only a few public addresses in one day. Second, only voters who are interested in an election pay attention to the candidate's address.

From the standpoint of the number of voters contacted, a *candidate's face-to-face contact with voters* is also not effective, because a candidate can only contact a small number of voters face-to-face during the campaign period.

A *candidate's contact with voters through the mass media* is the method used to contact a large number of voters. Particularly, this is the most important and the only effective method for contacting voters in high-profile elections, such as presidential and governor's elections. Meanwhile this method is not always available to low-profile elections, such as the local election. In elections in the United States, where the local mass media is well developed, and where the media are available for the campaign even in a low-profile election, many voters can be contacted through the mass media.

However, in elections in many nations, such as Korea, where the local mass media are not well developed, a candidate cannot reach voters through the mass media.

From the standpoint of the number of voters contacted, *canvassers' contact with voters face-to-face or by phone* is an effective method, because at least several dozen canvassers contact voters in a low-profile election and several hundred canvassers contact voters in a high-profile election. Some candidates running for the parliamentary election in Korea contacted all households in the district by telephone twice during the official campaign period of 16 days.

(b) When Voters Show Positive Responses to Campaign Activities

It may not be true that campaign activities can always draw positive responses from contacted voters. The following cases indicate when voters are more likely to respond positively to campaign activities.

① Voters, who are contacted by the candidate or his/her canvassers on the voters' initiative, tend to show a positive response, because these voters are usually interested in campaign activities. In contrast, it is difficult for voters to be positive when they are contacted unexpectedly, because these voters are likely to have little interest in, or to be disenchanted by the campaign.

② Voters are also likely to show a positive response when they are contacted by candidates rather than canvassers, because candidates deliver their image to these voters when they contact the voters, whereas canvassers cannot do so.

Table 9.2 When the probability of voters' showing a positive response to campaign activities is high

	When voters are contacted by the candidate or canvassers on the voters' initiative	When voters are unexpectedly contacted by the candidate or canvassers
When voters are contacted by the candidate	High probability of showing a positive response	Middle in probability of showing a positive response
When voters are contacted by canvassers	Middle in probability of showing a positive response	Low probability of showing a positive response

Table 9.2 indicates when the probability of voters' showing a positive response to campaign activities is high, considering the two criteria described above at the same time.

① The probability of voters' showing a positive response to campaign activities is high when they are contacted by the candidate on their own initiative.

② The probability of voters' showing positive response is in the middle when voters are unexpectedly contacted by the candidate, and when voters are contacted by canvassers on the voters' initiative.

③ The probability of voters' showing positive response is low when voters are unexpectedly contacted by canvassers.

In the following, each campaign method is evaluated based on the criteria described above.

A candidate's public address is high in probability of drawing positive responses from voters for the following reasons. The first is that only voters who intend to listen to a candidate's address pay attention the address. The second is that candidates can ask for support from voters by delivering their image when they make a speech.

A candidate's face-to-face contact with voters is in the middle in probability of drawing positive responses from voters for two reasons. Candidates usually contact voters face-to-face, regardless of the voters' desire to be contacted, in which case this method may not be so effective in getting a positive response. However, candidates can ask for support from voters by delivering their image when they contact voters, in which case this method may be effective.

A candidate's contact with voters through the mass media is high in probability of drawing positive responses from voters for the following reasons. First, only voters who are interested in elections pay attention to campaign advertisements in the mass media. Second, a candidate can deliver his/her image to voters to some degree through the mass media.

Canvassers' contact with voters face-to-face or by telephone is low in probability of drawing positive responses from voters for two reasons. First, this method is done regardless of the voters' intention to be contacted. Second, canvassers cannot deliver the candidate's image with this method.

(c) Overall Evaluation of Campaign Methods and their Effective Use

In Table 9.3, the effectiveness of each method is compared in terms of resources needed in addition to the number of voters contacted, and the probability of drawing positive responses from voters.

Table 9.3 Evaluation of campaign methods

Campaign method	Number of contacted voters	Probability of drawing positive response	Amount of required resources
Candidate's public address	Few	High	Little
Candidate's face-to-face contact with voters	Few	Middle	Little
Candidate's contact with voters through the mass media	Great many	High	Very much
Canvassers' contact with voters face-to-face or by telephone	Many	Low	Much

A candidate's public address and a *candidate's face-to-face contact with voters* are good methods for obtaining positive responses from voters, but are very limited methods in terms of the number of voters contacted. Therefore, they are only effective in getting votes in low-profile elections, such as the mayoral election in a small city. As seen in Table 9.4, these methods are suggested to be used primarily for getting support from the most crucial voters among the *target voters*. These can be also used for increasing voters' recognition of a candidate and raising the voting rates of the candidate's supporters.

A *candidate's contact with voters through the mass media* is the method used to contact numerous voters and to draw positive responses from the voters. Since this method costs candidates a great deal of money, it is used at the point of time that *target voters* are most interested in elections. As seen in ·Table 9.4, this method is suggested primarily for getting support from the *target voters*. This can also be used for increasing voters' recognition of a candidate and raising the voting rates of the candidate's supporters.

Canvassers' contact with voters face-to-face or by telephone is the method used to contact a large number of voters. However, this method may not be very good in getting positive response from voters. Voters are likely to welcome the request for help from the canvassers of the candidate whom they already support. Therefore, as seen in Table 9.4, this method is suggested to be used mainly for increasing voters' recognition of a candidate and for raising the voting rate of the candidate's supporters.

Table 9.4 Proper use of campaign methods

Campaign method	Increasing voters' recognition of a candidate	Obtaining support from target voters	Raising the voting rate of the candidate's supporters
Candidate's public address & Candidate's face-to-face contact with voters	X	X	X
Candidate's contact with voters through the mass media	X	X	X
Canvassers' contact with voters face-to-face or by telephone	X	△	X

(3) Inspecting the Effectiveness of Each Campaign Method

The effectiveness of each campaign method is generally evaluated in Table

9.4 above. However, it may not be possible to apply this evaluation to all electoral districts. Therefore, it is desirable for a candidate to closely examine the effectiveness of each campaign method in his/her district before the campaign begins.

The following is a real example of inspecting the effectiveness of each campaign method in a district for a parliamentary member in Seoul, Korea in 1996 based on a private survey,[20] which was conducted for Candidate Tae. S. Lee, who was running for the upcoming parliamentary election.

(a) *Candidate's Public Address*

Respondents were asked the question, *"Did you attend one of the candidates' public addresses in the last parliamentary election?"* As seen in Table 9.5, 24.4% of the total respondents answered, *"Yes"*; 75.6% answered, *"No."* This meant that around one fourth of the total voters had attended at least one candidate's address in the last parliamentary election in that district.

Table 9.5 Responses to the question, *"Did you attend one of the candidates' public addresses in the last parliamentary election?"*

Yes	No
24.4%	75.6%

Respondents who had attended a candidate's public address were asked, *"After attending a candidate's public address, did you come to like that candidate more than before or not?"* Table 9.6 shows that 20% of the respondents answered that they had come to *"Like the candidate more than before"*; 4.4% said they had come to *"Hate the candidate more than before"*; 62.6% said there had been *"No change in their feelings"*; 13% said that their feelings were *"Different according to candidates"* whom they had met. This

---

[20] Sample size of this survey is 1,105

meant that the candidate's public address had been a successful campaign method for getting positive response from voters in the last parliamentary election in this district.

A voter's coming to have positive feelings for a candidate does not necessarily mean that he/she will cast a vote for the candidate. Granted that all voters coming to have positive feelings for a candidate cast votes for that candidate, candidates could get support from only around 4.9% of the total voters through public addresses in this district.

The number of the main candidates in the last election in this district had been two. Consequently, the number of voters from whom each candidate could obtain support through public addresses in the upcoming parliamentary election might not be over an average of 2.5% of the total voters.

Table 9.6 Responses to the question, *"After attending a public address, did you come to like or hate the candidate more than before or not?"* (**Asked only to respondents who said** *"Yes"* **in Table 9.5**)

Liked more than before	Hated more than before	No change in feelings	Different according to candidates
20%	4.4%	62.6%	13%
(4.9% of total respondents)	(1.1% of total respondents)	(15.3% of total respondents)	(3.2% of total respondents)

Respondents who said that they had come to like or hate the candidate after attending the public address were asked, *"Why did you come to like or hate the candidate?"* While a particular reason for coming to hate the candidate more than before was not found, Table 9.7 shows some reasons of coming to like him/her more than before. As seen in the table, 29.6% of the respondents answered, *"Liked the candidate's public commitments"*; another 29.6% answered, *"Came to know the candidate"*; 11.1% answered, *"Liked the candidate's image"*; 7.4% answered, *"Attitude of working hard."* This meant that voters had paid attention to a candidate's commitments and image in the last election in this district. Therefore, candidates in this district had to thoroughly research commitments and images that voters wanted, and delivered them to voters in their speeches in the upcoming parliamentary election.

Table 9.7 Responses to the question, *"Why did you come to like or hate him/her?"* (Asked only to respondents who said *"Liked or hated more than before"* in Table 9.6)

Reason for coming to like the candidate	100%
Liked the candidate's public commitments	29.6% (1.3% of total respondents)
Came to know the candidate	29.6% (1.3% of total respondents)
Liked the candidate's image	11.1% (0.4% of total respondents)
Attitude of working hard	7.4% (0.3% of total respondents)
Other	22.3% (1% of total respondents)

(b) *Candidate's Face-to-Face Contact with Voters*

The question, *"Were you contacted face-to-face by any candidate in the last parliamentary election?"* was asked of respondents. As seen in Table 9.8, 28.6% of the total respondents answered that they had met one of the candidates face-to-face. This meant that a little more than one fourth of the total voters had met at least one candidate in the last parliamentary election in this district.

Table 9.8 Responses to the question, *"Were you contacted face-to-face by any candidate in the last parliamentary election?"*

Yes	No	Total
28.6%	71.4%	100%

Voters who had met candidates face-to-face in the last election were asked the question, *"After your meeting with the candidate, did you come to like him/her more than before or not?"* As seen in Table 9.9, 27.2% of the respondents answered that they had come to *"Like the candidate more than before"*; 1.3% said they had come to *"Hate the candidate more than before"*; 62% said there had been *"No change in their feelings"*; 9.5% said that their feelings were *"Different according to candidates"* whom they had met. This meant that candidates' face-to-face contact with voters had been a successful campaign method for getting positive response from voters in the last parliamentary election in this district.

Table 9.9 Responses to the question, *"After your meeting with the candidate, did you come to like or hate him/her more than before or not?"* (Asked only to respondents who said *"Yes"* in Table 9.8)

Liked more than before	Hated more than before	No change in feelings	Different according to candidates
27.2%	1.3%	62%	9.5%
(7.7% of total respondents)	(0.3% of total respondents)	(17.9% of total respondents)	(2.7% of total respondents)

Granted that all voters coming to have positive feelings for a candidate cast votes for that candidate, candidates could get support from only around 7.7% of the total voters with face-to-face contact in this district. The number of the main candidates in the last parliamentary election in this district had been two; consequently, the number of voters from whom each candidate could obtain support with his/her face-to-face contact in the upcoming parliamentary election might not be over an average of 4% of the total voters.

Table 9.10 Responses to the question, *"Why did you come to like or hate him/her more than before?"* **(Asked only to respondents who said** *"Liked or hated more than before"* **in Table 9.9)**

Reason for coming to like him/her more than before	100%
Feeling close	26.7% (2.06% of total respondents)
Attitude of working hard	18.6% (1.3% of total respondents)
Feeling confident in the candidate	10.5% (0.74% of total respondents)
Good looks of the candidate	9.3% (0.65% of total respondents)
Other	34.9% (2.44% of total respondents)

Respondents who answered that they had come to like or hate the candidate after face-to-face contact with him/her were asked the question, *"Why did you come to like or hate him/her more than before?"* While no particular reason for coming to hate the candidate more than before was not found, Table 9.10 shows some reasons of coming to like him/her more than before. As seen in the table, 26.7% of the respondents said, *"Feeling close";* 18.6% answered, *"Attitude of working hard";* 10.5% answered, *"Feeling confident in the candidate";* 9.3% answered, "Good looks of the candidate."

This meant that candidates' face-to-face contact with voters had been a successful campaign method in getting positive response from voters in the last parliamentary election in this district.

A notable point was that reasons for coming to like the candidate more than before were all related to the candidates' images. This suggested that candidates must do their best in transmitting their good image to voters when they met voters face-to-face in the upcoming parliamentary election in this district.

(c) *Canvassers' Face-to-Face Contact with Voters*

Respondents were asked the question, *"Were you contacted face-to-face by any canvasser in the last parliamentary election?"* Table 9.11 shows that 58.7% of the total respondents answered, *"Yes"* and 41.3% answered, *"No."* This meant that canvassers had been considerably effective in contacting voters quantitatively.

Table 9.11 Responses to the question, *"Were you contacted face-to-face by any canvasser in the last parliamentary election?"*

Yes	No
58.7%	41.3%

Respondents who had met canvassers face-to-face were asked, *"After your meeting with the canvasser, did you come to like the candidate the canvasser was promoting more than before or not?"* Table 9.12 shows that 4% of the respondents answered that they had come to *"Like the candidate more than before"*; 6.2% said they had come to *"Hate the candidate more than before"*; 87.2% said there had been *"No change in their feelings"*; 2.6% said that their feelings were *"Different according to candidates."* This result meant that canvassers' face-to-face contact with voters rarely changed voters' choice in the last parliamentary election in this district.

Table 9.12 Responses to the question, *"After your meeting with the canvasser, did you come to like or hate the candidate the canvasser was promoting more than before?"* (Asked only to respondents who said *"Yes"* in Table 9.11)

Liked more than before	Hated more than before	No change in feelings	Different according to candidates
4%	6.2%	87.2%	2.6%
(2.3% of total respondents)	(3.6% of total respondents)	(51.1% of total respondents)	(1.5% of total respondents)

Respondents who answered that they had come to like a candidate after being contacted by canvassers were asked, *"Why did you come to like him/her?"* Table 9.13 shows that 26.9% of the respondents said, *"Came to know the candidate"*; 15.4% answered, *"Feeling close"*; 11.5% said, *"Attitude of working hard"*; another 11.5% answered, *"Feeling confident."*

Respondents who answered that they had come to hate a candidate after being contacted by canvassers were asked, *"Why did you come to hate him/her?"* Table 9.13 shows that 82.5% of the respondents said, *"Excessive campaign activities"*; 10% answered, *"spoke ill of other candidates."*

Table 9.13 Responses to the question, *"Why did you come to like or hate the candidate?"* (Asked only to respondents who said *"Liked or hated more than before"* in Table 9.12)

Reason for coming to like the candidate more than before		Reason for coming to hate the candidate more than before	
Came to know the candidate	26.9% (1% of total respondents)	Excessive campaign activities	82.5% (3.1% of total respondents)
Feeling close	15.4% (0.6% of total respondents)	Spoke ill of other candidates	10% (0.6% of total respondents)
Attitude of working hard	11.5% (0.5% of total respondents)	Other	7.5% (0.5% of total respondents)
Feeling confident in the candidate	11.5% (0.5% of total respondents)		
Other	34.7% (1.3% of total respondents)		

In sum, candidates must be very careful in using canvassers' face-to-face contact with voters in the upcoming parliamentary election in this district. Before using this method, candidates must educate their canvassers not to be very active in asking for support and not to abuse the other candidates.

(d) *Canvassers' Telephone Contact with Voters*

Respondents were asked the question, *"Did you receive a phone call from any canvassers asking you to support the candidate he/she was promoting in the last parliamentary election?"* Table 9.14 shows that 39.2% of the voters answered, *"Yes"* and 60.8% answered, *"No."* This meant that canvassers were somewhat effective in contacting voters quantitatively in the last parliamentary election in this district.

Table 9.14 Responses to the question, *"Did you receive a phone call from any canvassers asking you to support the candidate he/she was promoting in the last parliamentary election?"*

Yes	No
39.2%	60.8%

Respondents whom canvassers had contacted by telephone were asked, *"After you were contacted by the canvasser, did you come to like or hate the candidate the canvasser was promoting more than before?"* Table 9.15 shows that 8.1% of the respondents answered that they had come to *"Like the candidate more than before"*; 24% said they had come to *"Hate the candidate more than before"*; 63.7% said there had been *"No change in their feelings"*; 4.2% said that their feelings had been *"Different according to candidates."* This meant that canvassers' contact with voters by telephone had been a

Table 9.15 Responses to the question, *"After you were contacted by the canvasser, did you come to like or hate the candidate the canvasser was promoting more than before?"* (Asked only to respondents who said *"Yes"* in Table 9.14)

Liked more than before	Hated more than before	No change in feelings	Different according to candidates
8.1%	24%	63.7%	4.2%
(3.1% of total respondents)	(9.4% of total respondents)	(25% of total respondents)	(1.6% of total respondents)

considerably negative influence on voters and could even be a cause of defeat in the last parliamentary election in this district.

Respondents who answered that they had come to like a candidate after being contacted by canvassers were asked, *"Why did you come to like him/her?"* Table 9.16 shows that 28.6% of the respondents said, *"Attitude of working very hard"*; 22.9% answered, *"Came to know the candidate"*; 11.4% said, *"Liked the candidate's image"*; 8.6% answered, *"Liked the candidate's politeness."*

Respondents who answered that they had come to hate a candidate after being contacted by canvassers were asked, *"Why did you come to hate him/her?"* Table 9.16 shows that 57.7% of the respondents said, *"Excessive campaign activities"*; 12% answered, *"Spoke ill of other candidates."*

The results above suggested that it was better for candidates not to use the canvassers' telephone contact with voters in the upcoming parliamentary election in this district. If candidates wanted to use this method, they would have to educate their canvassers not to be very active in asking for support and not to abuse other candidates.

Table 9.16 Responses to the question, *"Why did you come to like or hate the candidate?"* (Asked only to respondents who said *"Liked or hated more than before"* in Table 9.15)

Reason for coming to like the candidate more than before		Reason for coming to hate the candidate more than before	
Attitude of working very hard	28.6% (0.9% of total respondents)	Excessive campaign activities	57.7% (9.4% of total respondents)
Came to know the candidate	22.9% (0.7% of total respondents)	Spoke ill of other candidates	12% (1.1% of total respondents)
Liked the candidate's image	11.4% (0.4% of total respondents)	Other	30.3% (2.8% of total respondents)
Liked the candidate's politeness	8.6% (0.3% of total respondents)		
Other	28.5% (0.9% of total respondents)		

(e) Overall Evaluation of the Methods to Contact Voters in this District

Table 9.17 shows that methods to contact voters are evaluated in terms of the number of contacted voters out of the total number of voters, the number of voters in favor of the candidate after they are contacted, and the amount of material and personal resources needed for each method.

Table 9.17 Overall evaluations of methods to contact voters

Campaign method	Number of contacted voters of the total voters	Number of voters in favor of the candidate of the total voters	Amount of required resources
Candidate's public address	24.4%	15.6%	Little
Candidate's face-to-face contact with voters	28.6%	25.9%	Little
Canvassers' face-to-face contact with voters	58.7%	-2.2%	Much
Canvassers' telephone contact with voters	39.2%	-15.9%	Much

① *Candidate's public address and candidate's face-to-face contact with voters* had been somewhat effective in the last parliamentary election in this district. The reason was that voters rated these methods highly in favor of the candidates. Furthermore, they cost candidates a relatively small amount of resources. The only problem of these methods was that the number of contacted voters was relatively low. Therefore, these methods were suggested to be used for getting support from the most crucial *target voters* in the upcoming parliamentary election in this district.

② *Canvassers' face-to-face contact with voters* and *canvassers' telephone contact with voters* might not be an effective method because voters rated these methods negatively in terms of changing their mind in favor of the candidate in the last parliamentary election in this district. Furthermore, these methods cost the candidates a relatively large amount of resources. The only positive aspect of these methods was that the number of contacted voters was relatively high. Therefore, if a candidate wanted to use these methods, he/she must recruit canvassers of quality and train them well before canvassing, in order to increase the rate of voters in favor of a candidate. These methods were also suggested to be used for increasing voters' recognition of the candidates rather than getting support from voters in the upcoming parliamentary election in this district.

2. Oral Transmission among Voters

Oral transmission is a phenomenon of transfer of information among voters. Its contents are usually made and initiated by candidates or the mass media. However, oral transmission spreads out spontaneously by voters in the next stage.

(1) Five Reasons why Oral Transmission among Voters is Important in a Campaign

① Since oral transmitters usually add their subjective view to facts that they transmit, they have influence on the receptors.

② Oral transmitters usually have a very close relationship with the receptors. Therefore, their oral transmission is very persuasive to the receptors.

③ Once a person participates in favorable oral transmission of a certain candidate, he/she tends to cast a vote for that candidate.

④ Oral transmission spreads spontaneously; hence, it costs the candidate very little.

⑤ It is very difficult to grasp how much a certain oral transmission spreads. Consequently, it is very difficult for a candidate harmed by that oral transmission to prepare proper countermeasures.

(2) Kinds of Elections and Importance of Oral Transmission

The degree of the importance of oral transmission among voters differs depending on the kinds of elections. In high-profile elections like presidential elections in which the mass media is widely used, oral transmission is very influential on voters' voting behavior. In detail, a large number of voters who watched television advertisements by candidates and debates between the candidates influence others by talking about what they saw on television and what they felt.

On the other hand, in low-profile elections like a small city mayoral election, oral transmission plays a far less important role than high-profile elections. To put it more specifically, the mass media have less interest in low-profile elections than high-profile elections; then, voters do not have much chance to get information about the candidates and the election through the mass media. As a result, voters' lack of information leads to oral transmission that is not very lively. In these low-profile elections, voters participate in oral transmission only when the content of oral transmission is of interest to other voters.

(3) Characteristics of Successful Oral Transmission

A great deal of oral transmission usually reaches voters at the same time to draw their attention to a particular candidate. Therefore, an oral transmission must be superior to others in attracting voters' attention. Figure 9.1 shows conditions necessary for a successful oral transmission.

Figure 9.1 Conditions necessary for a successful oral transmission

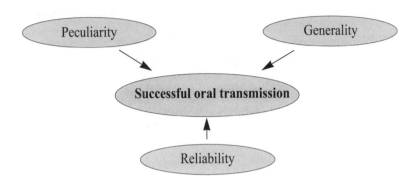

(a) Peculiarity

Content of oral transmission must be peculiar enough to induce voters' interest.

(b) Reliability

Content of oral transmission must be reliable. For this, it should be provided with clear evidence or its transmitters have to be trustworthy.

(c) Generality

Content of oral transmission has to be related to many people's interests. Oral transmission is apt to be particularly explosive, when it is directly related to the dissatisfaction or curiosity of most voters.

(4) Kinds of Voters and their Oral Transmission

(a) *Fixed Supporters*

These are voters who strongly support a certain candidate. Consequently, they always try to talk with other voters about the strong points of the candidate whom they support. They also attempt to refute other voters' oral transmission against the candidate whom they support.

(b) *Fluid Supporters*

These are voters who support a candidate now, but may support other candidates if the situation changes. In other words, they are a candidate's weak supporters. They tend to talk to other voters about the strong points of the candidate whom they support, only when it is certain that other voters will not refute them.

(c) Undecided Voters

These are voters who have not decided yet for whom they will vote. In the early stages of the campaign period, they are apt to receive oral transmission from others rather than participate in it themselves. However, in the last stage of the campaign period, they sometimes become oral transmitters.

Undecided voters' oral transmission is very powerful, for two reasons. First, because they participate in oral transmission only when they have irrefutable evidence and proper logic for it. Hence, it is difficult to stop their oral transmission, just like a communicable disease without a vaccine. Second, their oral transmission has particularly great impact on other undecided voters, who would rather not listen to voters who have already decided for whom they will vote, but will listen to advice from undecided voters.

(5) Selection of Oral Transmitters

In order to effectively get votes, candidates should select and use appropriate oral transmitters from the early stages of the campaign period. Two kinds of oral transmitters are described below.

(a) *Trusted Oral Transmitters*

These are persons respected by other voters. They include a leader of a group or village and the head of a family. Their oral transmission is very powerful because it contains their authoritative interpretation on the content of oral transmission. Once they start the oral transmission, ordinary transmitters described below are able to perpetuate their message. However, it is very difficult to find *trusted oral transmitters* in urban districts.

(b) *Ordinary Oral Transmitters*

These are persons who are acknowledged as having much information by others because they have many contacts with various people in the district or they are highly interested in elections. However, since they are not respected by others or are not well educated, their interpretation of the content of oral transmission is not easily acceptable to others. Then, they tend to transmit only facts to others. In a district where *trusted oral transmitters* are rarely found, a candidate should use *ordinary oral transmitters* for getting votes.

(6) Method for Computing an Oral Transmission Index

Candidates must always grasp how much voters communicate about them. In the following, the method for computing the degree of oral transmission among voters about each candidate is described.

Oral transmission can be divided into two. One is active oral transmission that is about how many voters talk to other voters about a certain candidate. The other is passive oral transmission that is about how many voters listen to other voters about a certain candidate.

(a) Method for Computing a Weekly Active Oral Transmission Index

The following questions must be asked to respondents in a private survey for computing a weekly active oral transmission index for a candidate running for an election.

Q1) *"Have you talked to other voters about any candidate running for the upcoming election during the last 7 days?"*

(1) *Yes, I have*   (2) *No, I have not*

Q1.1) (Ask only to respondents who answer *"Yes"* in Q1) *"Then, which candidate have you talked about?"*

(1) *Candidate A*   (2) *Candidate B*   (3) *Both*

Q1.1.1) (Ask only to respondents who answer *"Candidate A"* or *"Candidate B"* in Q1.1) *"Was the content of your discussions about the candidate positive or negative?"*

(1) *Positive*   (2) *Negative*   (3) *Neutral*

Q1.1.2) (Ask only to respondents who answer *"Both"* in Q1.1) *"Was the content of your discussions about the candidates positive or negative?"*

For Candidate A: (1) *Positive*   (2) *Negative*   (3) *Neutral*

For Candidate B: (1) *Positive*   (2) *Negative*   (3) *Neutral*

■ Formula of a Weekly Active Oral Transmission Index

Weekly active oral transmission index for Candidate A=% of voters talking about Candidate A x (% of positive -% of negative)/100

If we want the specific content of the discussions in which oral transmitters participated, we must ask them the following question.

Q1.2) (Ask to only respondents who answer *"Yes"* in Q1) *"Would you tell me specifically what you were saying about the candidate?"*

For Candidate A (   )

For Candidate B (   )

(b) Method for Computing a Weekly Passive Oral Transmission Index

The following questions must be asked to respondents in a private survey for computing a weekly passive oral transmission index for a candidate running for an election.

Q2) *"Have you listened to other voters about any candidate running for the upcoming election during the last 7 days?"*

(1) *Yes, I have*   (2) *No, I have not*

Q2.1) (Ask only to respondents who answer *"Yes"* in Q2) *"Then, which candidate have you heard about?"*

(1) *Candidate A*   (2) *Candidate B*   (3) *Both*

Q2.1.1) (Ask only to respondents who answer *"Candidate A"* or *"Candidate B"* in Q2.1) *"Is the content of what you heard about the candidate positive or negative?"*

(1) *Positive* (2) *Negative* (3) *Neutral*

Q2.1.2) (Ask only to respondents who answer *"Both"* in Q 2.1) *"Is the content of what you heard about the candidates positive or negative?"*

For Candidate A: (1) *Positive* (2) *Negative* (3) *Neutral*

For Candidate B: (1) *Positive* (2) *Negative* (3) *Neutral*

■ Formula of a Weekly Passive Oral Transmission Index

Weekly passive oral transmission index for Candidate A = % of voters hearing about Candidate A x (% of positive - % of negative)/100

If we want the specific content of what voters heard, we must ask them the following question.

Q2.2) (Ask only respondents who answer *"Yes"* in Q2) *"Would you tell me specifically what you have heard about each candidate?"*

For Candidate A: ( )

For Candidate B: ( )

(c) Method for Measuring the Total Oral Transmission Index

■ Formula of a Weekly Total Oral Transmission Index

Weekly total oral transmission index for Candidate A= Weekly active oral transmission index for Candidate A + Weekly passive oral transmission index for Candidate A

(7) Hypothetical Example of an Oral Transmission Index

Table 9.18 shows the oral transmission index of supporters for Candidate A and Candidate B and undecided voters. The active oral transmission index of *fixed supporters* of both Candidate A and Candidate B are the same at 80. The passive oral transmission index of *fixed supporters* of both Candidate A and Candidate B are also the same at 20.

Table 9.18 Hypothetical example of an oral transmission index

Kinds of voter	Fixed supporter		Fluid supporter		Undecided voter	
Candidate	A	B	A	B	A	B
Active oral transmission index	80	80	50	20	10	-2
Passive oral transmission index	20	20	40	-10	40	-50
Total oral transmission index	100	100	90	10	50	-52

* The maximum value of total oral transmission index is 200

There is a clear difference in the oral transmission index of *fluid supporters* between Candidate A and Candidate B. The active oral transmission index of *fluid supporters* for Candidate A is 50, while that for Candidate B is only 20.

The passive oral transmission index of *fluid supporters* for Candidate A is 40, whereas that for Candidate B is-10. The sum of the oral transmission index of *fluid supporters* for Candidate A is 90, while that for Candidate B is only 10.

The result above means that Candidate A's *fluid supporters* have talked about Candidate A and heard many positive things about Candidate A. Meanwhile, Candidate B's *fluid supporters* have not talked much about Candidate B, and they have received negative information about him/her.

There is also a clear difference in the oral transmission index of undecided voters. The active oral transmission index of undecided voters about Candidate A is 10, while that about Candidate B is -2. This means that some of the undecided voters have started active oral transmission for Candidate A.

The passive oral transmission index of undecided voters about Candidate A is 40, while that about Candidate B is -50. This means that favorable oral transmission for Candidate A is delivered to undecided voters, while unfavorable oral transmission against Candidate B is conveyed to undecided voters.

Given the trend in Table 9.18, we can forecast that most undecided voters would vote for Candidate A rather than Candidate B. While most of Candidate A's *fluid supporters* will vote for Candidate A, a considerable number of Candidate B's *fluid supporters* will give up supporting Candidate B. Therefore, support for Candidate A will rise; support for Candidate B will drop.

Chapter 10
Use of Election Surveys

1. Necessity of Election Surveys for Scientific Campaign Strategies

Scientific campaign strategies are based on objective and proper information, while unscientific campaign strategies are based on subjective and unreliable information. Thus, scientific strategies increase the probability of winning, because they help candidates get votes effectively, while unscientific strategies, which lead a candidate to campaign based on wrong interpretations of core conditions affecting the election, can be a direct cause of electoral defeat.

Election surveys are one of crucial tools necessary to obtain objective and reliable information for scientific campaign strategies. They provide basic information, such as voters' recognition of, and support for candidates.

2. Principal Terms of Surveys Related to Campaign Strategies

(1) Voters' Recognition of Candidates

Voters' recognition of candidates is about how well known a candidate is. Voters' recognition is very important in a district where most voters cast their votes based on their evaluation of candidates' images and careers. Then, in such a district, candidates have to make sure that voters recognize their name, image, and career before everything else.

However, candidates' images and careers are not important to voters who vote based on their evaluation of political parties. For example, in a district composed of Area A and Area B, if all voters in Area A vote for Party X and all voters in Area B vote for Party Y owing to strong confrontation between the two areas, then the voters' recognition of candidates is not an important factor in getting votes.

Voters' recognition of candidates can be divided into three kinds: *unaided recall, top-of-the-mind recall,* and *aided recall.*

(a) *Unaided Recall*

This refers to respondents' ability to extract names of candidates from their memory without seeing a list of the names of the candidates. It is usually asked in the following form.

Q1) *"Do you recognize the names of the candidates who are running for the congressional district in which you are currently living?"*

Voters who can recall a candidate's name and also show their support for the candidate are highly likely to vote for him/her on Election Day. In the meantime, there is high likelihood that voters who recall a candidate's name, but do not support the candidate, do not vote for the candidate on Election Day.

(b) *Top-of-the-Mind Recall*

This refers to respondents' ability to recall a candidate's name first in response to an open-ended question asking them to recall the names of more than two candidates, without giving them a list of the names of the candidates. The form of question used to measure *top-of-the-mind recall* is the same as that for *unaided recall.*

Voters recalling more than two candidates' names are ones who are usually somewhat interested in politics or who are well-educated. Voters are likely to vote for the candidate whose name they recall first, because they tend to recall first the candidate whom they like best.

(c) *Aided Recall*

This refers to respondents' ability to recall a candidate's name in a closed-ended question in which a candidate's name appears. It may be true that voters who make *aided recall* tend to have less interest in the election than voters who make *unaided recall*. Undecided voters are more easily found among voters who make only *aided recall*. In the meantime, a candidate's *fixed supporters* and *fluid supports* are easily found among voters who make *unaided recall*. The question is usually asked in the following form.

Q2) *"Have you heard about Candidate A running for the congressional district in which you are currently living?"*

(1) Yes   (2) No

Q2.1) (Ask to only respondents who said *"Yes"* in Q2) *"How well do you know the candidate?"*

(1) *Have heard only the candidate's name*

(2) *Have heard both the candidate's name and about his/her career*

(3) *Have known a lot about the candidate*

Recognizing only a candidate's name may not be a sufficient condition for supporting that candidate. As a rule, it is highly possible that voters vote for a candidate on Election Day when they know not only the candidate's name, but also something about his/her career.

(2) Voters' Recognition of Candidates in Different Elections

The general characteristics of voters' recognition of candidates are described below.

① Voters' recognition of candidates for the presidential election is usually the highest. In most democratic countries, voters' recognition of candidates is usually close to 100% on Election Day of a presidential election. Voters' recognition of candidates for the governor's or big city mayoral elections is second highest. Voters' recognition of candidates running for congressional member or a small city mayor is the lowest.

② Voters' recognition of candidates for elections in rural areas is usually higher than those in cities for the same kind of election, because voters in rural areas have more interest in an election than those living in cities.

③ Voters in rural areas recognize candidates in more detail than those living in cities. Those living in rural areas usually know even a candidate's career, while the greater part of those living in cities just recognize the candidates' names.

(3) Support for a Candidate

This is the foremost important concept for campaign strategies and is divided into *comparative support* and *non-comparative support.*

(a) *Comparative Support*

As seen in Question 3, comparative support measures support for each candidate when the names of all of the candidates are supplied in the question. Therefore, we can immediately know each candidate's probability of victory at a given point of time.

Q3) *"Whom will you support, if Candidates A, B, and C run for the congressional district in which you are currently living?"*

(1) *Candidate A*   (2) *Candidate B*

(3) *Candidate C*   (4) *Don't know*

(b) *Non-Comparative Support*

As seen in Question 4, *non-comparative support* measures support for a certain candidate when the names of his/her opponents are not given in the question. It is usually used for an incumbent candidate when his/her opponents are yet unknown. For Question 4, respondents who answer *"Will surely support"* are likely to be Candidate A's *fixed supporters*; respondents who answer *"Will probably support"* are likely to be Candidate A's *fluid supporters.*

Q4) *"Will you support Candidate A, the incumbent congressional member of your district, if he/she comes forward as a candidate again in the upcoming election?"*

(1) *Will surely support*   (2) *Will probably support*

(3) *Will probably not support*   (4) *Will surely not support*

For a candidate, *non-comparative support* is usually higher than *comparative support*, because the former is measured without putting his/her opponents' names in the question.

A candidate's probability of victory based on *non-comparative support* can be roughly predicted as follows. When the number of voters who respond to support a candidate is greater than the sum of the undecided voters and the voters responding that they will not support him/her, the candidate's probability of victory is high. In other words, when *non-comparative support* for a candidate is more than 50%, he/she has a high probability of victory.

When the number of voters who respond to support a candidate is a little fewer than the sum of the voters who are undecided and who respond that they will not support him/her, the candidate's probability of victory is in the middle. More specifically, when *non-comparative support* for a candidate is between 40-50%, the candidate's probability of victory would be around 50%.

When the number of voters who respond that they will support a candidate is far fewer than the sum of the undecided voters and the voters responding that they will not support him/her, the candidate's probability of victory is usually low. Put another way, when *non-comparative support* for a candidate is less than 30%, he/she has a very low probability of victory.

(4) Preference

As seen in Question 5, this is measured to anticipate which candidate undecided voters will support.

Q5) (Ask only to respondents who answer *"Don't know"* in Q3) *"Which candidate do you prefer over others?"*

(1) *Candidate A*   (2) *Candidate B*

(3) *Candidate C*   (4) *Prefer no candidate*

(5) *Possibility of Victory*

This is about which candidate voters think will win in the election, regardless of whom they support. The purpose of this question is to measure the so-called *bandwagon effect*, which refers to voters' tendency to like to vote for a candidate whose chance of victory is very high. Question 6 asks respondents which candidate might win in the upcoming election.

Q6) *"Can you guess who will win in the upcoming election, regardless of which candidate you support?"*

(1) *Candidate A*   (2) *Candidate B*

(3) *Candidate C*   (4) *Don't know*

3. Kinds of Surveys for Candidates

(1) Vulnerability/Feasibility Surveys

Defeat in an election causes a great deal of mental anguish and material loss to defeated candidates and their families. Therefore, candidates must check the probability of winning through vulnerability/feasibility surveys before they decide to run. If a candidate's probability of getting elected is very low, he/she would be better off giving up his/her candidacy.

Vulnerability/feasibility surveys are usually carried out by candidates challenging the incumbent. However, on rare occasions, they are also conducted by the incumbent. These surveys are composed of questions to measure voters' recognition of, support for, and supporters' strength of support for candidates.

(2) Survey for a Campaign Organization

Conflict among members of a campaign organization often impedes the effectiveness of a campaign. Survey for a campaign organization is carried out for a candidate to understand the causes of conflict among organization members and to help the candidate to eliminate the conflict.

Procedure of the survey for a campaign organization is as follows.

① The interviewer must be an experienced campaign strategist.

② The interviewer must conduct face-to-face interviews with each member of a campaign organization, including the candidate, for about one hour each.

③ The interviewer must begin with questions prepared in advance. However, when the interviewer finds in the process of the interview that other things not in the prepared questions are very important, he/she can ignore the prepared questions.

④ In some cases, by asking interviewees questions about campaign strategies, an interviewer examines how much knowledge about campaign strategies interviewees have.

⑤ It is desirable to ask the same questions to all of the interviewees in order to detect differences in their answers.

Tae. S. Lee, who had been a three-time parliamentary member in a district in Seoul, Korea and had been defeated in the last parliamentary election, requested the author to do a survey for his campaign organization as part of his plan in 1997 for the upcoming parliamentary election. This survey was conducted with 15 questions asked to 13 core staff members and canvassers. The following questions were asked.

① Do you think that the campaign was effectively carried out in the last election?

② What was the strategy promoting Candidate Lee's image in the last election?

③ How did the campaign organization members generally evaluate Candidate Lee?

④ What was the voters' reaction to Candidate Lee after they had contact with him?

⑤ What was the voters' reaction to Candidate Lee's wife after they had contact with her?

⑥ Was Candidate Lee physically strong enough to campaign in the last election?

⑦ Was Candidate Lee's wife physically strong enough to campaign in the last election?

⑧ Did Candidate Lee have good communication skills to address the public?

⑨ Did Candidate Lee's wife have good communication skills to address the public?

⑩ What were Candidate Lee's weak points and strong points?

⑪ What were Candidate Lee's wife's weak points and strong points?

⑫ Was the number of canvassers enough for running an effective campaign?

⑬ Was there any conflict among the campaign organization members?

⑭ What were the main causes of Candidate Lee's defeat in the last election?

⑮ What is the probability of Candidate Lee's winning in the upcoming election?

(a) Results of the Survey

① The campaign had not been scientifically conducted in the last election.

· *Target voters* had not been scientifically established.

· There had not been any attempt to learn what kind of candidate image voters favor.

· There had not been any clear guidelines for the canvassers' campaign activities.

② Candidate Lee had had a fine personality, but had not reflected the campaign organization members' opinion on the campaign plan in the last election. Therefore, the campaign organization members not only had not set forth their views to him, but they also had not run a rigorous campaign.

③ Voters who had contacted Candidate Lee usually had tended to show friendly feelings toward him.

④ Candidate Lee had made a good public speech, but his wife had not done so. She had also been too chatty in the formal meeting with voters.

⑤ Candidate Lee had been physically strong enough so that he could campaign 12 hours a day, but his wife had not been so.

(b) Suggestions for the Upcoming Election

① Candidate Lee must make scientific campaign strategies, including establishing *target voters* on the basis of thorough research on the district.

② Candidate Lee must make an effort to reflect the campaign organization members' opinion in making his campaign strategies.

③ After establishing the direction of a campaign, Candidate Lee must clearly instruct the direction that the staff members and canvassers must take.

④ Candidate Lee must campaign 12 hours a day during the campaign period.

⑤ Candidate Lee's wife must be trained by an expert to improve her communication and public speaking skills.

(3) Benchmark Surveys

These are conducted in order to establish a long-time campaign plan once a candidate decides to run. Since these surveys are conducted in order to gather scores of specific information about voters and the district, the face-to-face interview, which includes normally 40 questions, is used, rather than the telephone interview, which includes around 10 questions. Benchmark surveys usually include the following items.

① Voters' recognition of each candidate

② Voters' support for each candidate

③ Supporters' strength of support for each candidate

④ Reasons of support for each candidate

⑤ Degree of each candidate's contribution to the development of the district

⑥ Political party that a voter is currently supporting

⑦ Candidate's image favored by voters

⑧ A route of oral transmission among voters

⑨ The candidate that a voter supported in the last election

⑩ The most important issues to be solved in the district

⑪ Evaluation of campaigns conducted by each candidate in the last election

(4) Follow-up Surveys

These are conducted by candidates in order to check the effectiveness of a campaign they have run and modify the campaign plan if there are mistakes in the campaign conducted during the campaign period. The face-to-face interview is normally used in follow-up surveys, since follow-up surveys examine many things as much as benchmark surveys. However, some candidates use the telephone interview, because it takes a shorter time and costs less than the face-to-face interview.

(5) Tracking Surveys

Tracking surveys are periodically conducted to grasp variations of voters' recognition of, and support for candidates. Therefore, the same questions are repeatedly asked in tracking surveys conducted in different periods.

Tracking surveys usually use the telephone interview, which takes 1-2 days, rather than the face-to-face interview, which takes around 2 weeks. During the campaign period when support for candidates can abruptly vary overnight, 2 weeks for the face-to-face interview is usually too long.

(a) Sampling Method of Tracking Surveys

In a presidential election, tracking surveys are conducted very frequently (weekly or daily) in order to monitor any shift in voters' support for candidates, and this costs candidates a great deal of money.

Sometimes, *rolling samples* are used to curtail expense. In detail, if a candidate wants a survey of 1,000 samples every week, he/she does not need to survey a new set of 1,000 samples every week. During the first week the candidate conducts a survey of 1,000 samples. During the next week, he/she just conducts a survey of 500 samples to be added to the 500 samples of the survey of the first week, discarding 500 out of the 1,000 samples of the survey of the first week. During the third week, the candidate again conducts a survey of 500 samples to be added to the 500 samples of the second week, removing the remaining 500 samples of the survey of the first week.

However, *rolling samples* have a weak point, which is that when a great change in support occurs overnight because of an unexpected accident, part of the *rolling samples* cannot be used to explain that change.

(b) When Tracking Surveys are Needless

① When voters are never interested in an election so that there is almost no variation in voters' recognition of, and support for candidates up to Election Day, tracking surveys are not necessary.

② When a candidate's campaign organization is so stiff that it is almost impossible for the organization to adapt to the updated plan based on the results of tracking surveys, tracking surveys are unnecessary.

(6) Panel Studies

These are a kind of tracking survey. However, they are different from tracking surveys, in that they ask questions to the same respondents in surveys conducted in different periods. Therefore, this survey method most clearly informs us of shifts in support between different periods.

Panel studies also have a drawback. Since in this method the same people are interviewed over again, they are repeatedly exposed to survey questions. Then, their characteristics are eventually changed to be different from those of normal people after they are exposed to surveys 3-4 times. Accordingly, their responses can no longer represent the population. The way to solve this problem is to change respondents after interviewing them 3-4 times.

(7) Focus Group Interview

This is the method that is used to gather opinion from 6 to 8 people in a room, who represent a broad demographic selection, under the direction of an experienced moderator for 1 to 2 hours. The moderator leads the participants to frankly set forth their views about certain topics.

The number of participants is only around 6 to 8; thus, their response cannot represent the view of all voters. However, because this method helps the candidate know what a participant is thinking, it is usually used when the candidate needs to know the voters' views about the candidate's image and policies and to find ways to upgrade them. In the following, a simple procedure executing this method is described.

(a) Selection of Participants

Selecting what kinds of people will participate in a focus group interview depends on the purpose of the study. For example, if the purpose of the study is to learn the voters' views about a certain candidate's image, it is better to select undecided voters as participants, because it is difficult for voters who have already decided to vote for a certain candidate to be objective in their evaluation of the candidate's image.

If possible, it is better to select people representing various demographic groups as participants. As seen Table 10.1, if the number of participants is 8, it is recommended to divide them equally into two groups by sex; after that, assign each person in the groups by their ages, such as 20s, 30s, 40s, and more than 50.

Table 10.1 Demographic groups of participants

	20s	30s	40s	More than 50
Male	1	1	1	1
Female	1	1	1	1

(b) Hypothetical Results of a Focus Group Interview

The following is an assumed example of the results of a focus group interview and description of their strategic use. Competing with Candidates B and C, Candidate A conducts a focus group interview to grasp which candidate is superior to others in political career, image, and scholastic ability.

Questions

The moderator asks questions to the participants in the following order.

① Which candidate is superior to others in each of political career, image, or scholastic ability?

② Which candidate is superior to others, considering political career and image simultaneously?

③ Which candidate is superior to others, considering political career and scholastic ability simultaneously?

④ Which candidate is superior to others, considering image and scholastic ability simultaneously?

⑤ Which candidate is superior to others, considering all three of political career, image, and scholastic ability simultaneously?

Results of Study and their Strategic Use for Each Candidate

① Candidate A appears to be superior to others only when career and scholastic ability are considered at the same time. Therefore, he/she must simultaneously emphasize his/her career and scholastic ability.

② Candidate B is revealed to be superior to others only in image. Therefore, he/she must emphasize only his/her image.

③ Candidate C appears to be superior to others when career, scholastic ability, and image are all considered at the same time or when only career is considered. If the remaining campaign period is very short, as much as around 15 days, it would be better for Candidate C to emphasize only his/her career rather than simultaneously stressing his/her career, scholastic ability, as well as image, because 15 days are not long enough to effectively stress all three. However, if the remaining campaign period is very long, as much as around one year, it would be better for Candidate C to emphasize his/her career, scholastic ability, as well as image at the same time, rather than stressing only his/her career, because one year is enough time to effectively stress all three aspects of the candidate.

(8) Push Polls

Push polls make voters favor a certain candidate over others by giving them favorable information about the candidate and unfavorable information about his/her opponents. There can be two kinds of push polls, depending on their purpose.

One kind of push poll is used when the candidate wants to increase voters' recognition of him/herself. It is mainly composed of questions related to a certain candidate, so it naturally makes the respondents recognize the candidate's name, career, and scholastic ability well in the process of responding to questions.

The second kind of push poll is used when the candidate wants to raise voters' support for him/herself. It usually provides positive information about the candidate and negative information about his/her opponents.

Push polls differ from other objective surveys in two respects. First, push polls usually ask fewer questions than other surveys. They are composed of at best 7-8 questions to lead the respondents to have a friendly feeling about a particular candidate, while other objective surveys consist of more than 10 objective questions. Second, push polls usually do not include demographic questions, while other objective surveys include such questions.

4. The Practical Use of Surveys

In my professional experience as campaign strategist in the last decade, I have arrived at some subjective views regarding when the first survey for a campaign should be conducted, how frequently surveys should be conducted, and what kind of survey company it is best to employ. I offer these views below.

(1) When should the First Survey for a Campaign be Conducted?

In a district where voters tend to decide whom they will support in the early stages of the campaign period, it is better to conduct the survey as early as possible, so that the campaign plan can be established early on. Voters who are well educated, older, or reside in rural areas tend to decide earlier than those who are poorly educated, younger, and reside in cities, because the former has more interest in politics than the latter. Meanwhile, in a district where voters tend to decide whom they will support in the last stage of the campaign period, it is fine if the survey is conducted a little later.

(2) How Frequently should Surveys be Conducted

The number of surveys that should be conducted for a campaign is not fixed. However, the following two factors must be considered in deciding how many surveys are usually conducted.

(a) Leading- or being behind in Candidate Support

A couple of surveys are enough for a candidate who is leading his/her opponents in support. Surveys are conducted just to confirm the candidate's steady lead in support. However, frequent surveys are necessary for a candidate who is behind his/her opponents in support, so that he/she can find ways to reverse the support.

(b) Rising- or Dropping in Candidate Support

Several surveys are sufficient for a candidate whose support has risen, because it is probable that his/her campaign strategy is on the right track. However, a candidate whose support has dropped must conduct many surveys to find reasons for the downward trend in his/her support and to reverse that trend.

Table 10.2 shows how frequently a certain candidate conducts surveys, simultaneously considering two factors described above, if the campaign period is less than one month. A candidate who leads others in support and whose support has risen needs just one or two surveys during the campaign period to confirm his/her lead in support.

Table 10.2 How many surveys are conducted in different conditions?

	A candidate leading in support	A candidate behind in support
A candidate rising in support	1-2 times	3-5 times
A candidate dropping in support	3-5 times	More than 8 times

It is recommended that both a candidate who leads others in support but whose support has dropped and a candidate who is behind others in support but whose support has risen conduct 3-5 surveys. The former needs to find out why his/her support has dropped; the latter has to learn when he/she catches up with the front-runner in support. A candidate behind his/her opponents in support and whose support has dropped must conduct more than 8 surveys. He/she needs to find ways to make his/her support rise.

(3) Selection of a Survey Company

Surveys for a campaign are conducted in order to grasp the state of an election and provide elementary but very important information necessary for devising effective strategies. Therefore, surveys must be conducted by pollsters who have considerable knowledge about campaign strategies. Only these pollsters can properly analyze and arrange data for campaign strategies.

Chapter 11
Interpretation and Analysis of an Election Survey

Accurate interpretations and analyses of election surveys are core requirements for devising effective campaign strategies. In fact, campaign strategies on the basis of wrong analysis of election surveys may cause a defeat in an election. It is, therefore, better for candidates to obtain advice from experts, who have experience and knowledge about both the survey and the campaign, when they interpret the results of an election survey. In the following, methods to interpret and analyze election surveys are described.

1. Interpretations of Election Surveys
(1) Considering Sampling Error when Interpreting Election Surveys
(a) Characteristics of the Sampling Error

Errors in survey findings are unavoidable, since election surveys are meant to measure voters' opinion on the basis of some voters subtracted from total voters. Table 11.1 shows sampling errors when the probability sampling method is used. When the sample size is 100, the sampling error is ±9.8%; when the sample size is 1,000, the sampling error is ±3.1%.

Table 11.1 Sampling errors with 95% confidence

Sample size	Sampling error	Gap of sampling error for +100 samples	Sample size	Sampling error	Gap of sampling error for +100 samples
100	±9.8%		600	±4.0%	-0.4%
200	±6.9%	-2.9%	700	±3.7%	-0.3%
300	±5.7%	-1.2%	800	±3.5%	-0.2%
400	±4.9%	-0.8%	900	±3.3%	-0.2%
500	±4.4%	-0.5%	1,000	±3.1%	-0.2%

As also seen in Table 11.1, when the sample size increases from 900 to 1,000, the sampling error decreases by only 0.2% from ±3.3% to ±3.1%. However, when the sample size increases from 100 to 200, the sampling error decreases by 2.9% from ±9.8% to ±6.9%. This shows that the gap of the sampling error is greater when adding 100 samples to a small sample than when adding 100 samples to a large sample.

(b) Considering Sampling Error when Interpreting Candidate Support

The sampling error must be carefully considered when interpreting candidate support, which is the most important in the results of a survey. Table 11.2 shows the results of a hypothetical survey with 600 samples, where support for Candidate A is indicated at 35% and support for Candidate B is indicated at 30%. However, we cannot interpret that Candidate A leads Candidate B by 5% in support.

Table 11.2 Determining range of support when considering sampling error

Candidate	Support	Sampling error (600 samples)	Range of support when considering sampling error
A	35%	±4%	31-39%
B	30%	±4%	26-34%

As indicated in Table 11.2, when the sample size is 600, the sampling error is ±4%. Applying ±4% to each candidate's support, support for Candidate A would be between 31% and 39% and support for Candidate B would be between 26% and 34%. The table indicates that part of the range of support for Candidate A is overlapped with that of support for Candidate B. As a result, it would be accurate to conclude that the two candidates are in close competition.

(c) Candidates' Tendency to Interpret the Candidate Support Inaccurately

Candidates usually like to overestimate support for themselves. Due to this wrong attitude, candidates think that they are in the lead without counting the sampling error when they lead in candidate support by more than 1%. However, they tend to count the sampling error when they are behind their opponents in support.

(2) Considering Sampling Error when Interpreting Tracking Surveys

When the results of tracking surveys are interpreted, it is not easy to know whether variation of candidate support in the tracking surveys is caused by the sampling error or whether there is real change in support. In fact, there is no clear way to solve this problem. The only way we can do is to estimate real variation in support as follows. When the variation of candidate support on tracking surveys is greater than the range of sampling errors, the minimum real variation in support is the number derived after sampling errors are subtracted from the variation of candidate support on tracking surveys.

Table 11.3 shows the results of hypothetical tracking surveys. Candidate A takes a survey two times in one month. The number of samples of the first survey is 1,100 and its sampling error is ±3%. The number of samples of the second survey is 600 and its sampling error is ±4%.

In the first survey, support for Candidate A is 20%; then, range of support for him/her after the sampling error is counted is between 17% and 23%.

Meanwhile, in the second survey, support for him/her is 30%; then, the range of support for him/her after the sampling error is counted is between 26% and 34%. Therefore, minimum variation of support for Candidate A, considering the sampling errors of both surveys, is +3%.

Table 11.3 Variation of support in the tracking surveys

Support in the 1st survey (Range)	Support in the 2nd survey (Range)	Variation of support on surveys	Minimum variation in support after sampling errors are counted
20% (17-23%)	30% (26-34%)	10%(30%-20%)	26% - 23% = 3%

(3) Method to Interpret Multiple Surveys Conducted in a Short Period of Time

Table 11.4 shows the results of three surveys with 600 samples each, conducted on Monday, Wednesday, and Friday of the same week, and these surveys reflect support for a candidate at 20%, 22%, and 24%. There are three methods to measure support for a candidate, given the results of three surveys.

Table 11.4 Hypothetical tracking surveys

	First survey (Monday)	Second survey (Wednesday)	Third survey (Friday)
Support	20%	22%	24%
Range of support when considering sampling error	16-24%	18-26%	20-28%

The first method of measurement is to use the average (22%) of the results of three surveys. The merit of this method is that since it uses the results of all three surveys, the sampling error is very low. More specifically, the sum of the samples of all three surveys is 1,800.

Therefore, its sampling error is only ±2.3%. Meanwhile, the drawback of this method is that it places the same weight on all three surveys, regardless of the time each survey was conducted. In other words, although the most recent survey tends to be more accurate than the others, this method ignores that fact.

The second method is to use only the results of the survey conducted on Friday, which is the most recent. Since this method is based on the most recent survey, it could be the most accurate. However, because it only uses 600 samples out of 1,800, its sampling error is ±4%, which is far greater than that of the first method.

The third method is to use the results of all of the surveys, placing different weights on the three surveys. In detail, the heaviest weight is placed on the most recent survey and the lightest weight is placed on the oldest survey. The third method tries to solve the drawbacks of the first and the second methods.

Since it uses the results of all three surveys, its sampling error is very low, by as much as ±2.3%. Because it puts more weight on the more recent survey, the third method increases the accuracy of the survey results. In fact, based on real tracking surveys conducted for 19 U.S. senate and governor's elections in 1996, the third method turned out to be the most accurate and the second method, the least accurate.[21]

(4) Analysis of Voters' Characteristics by Comparing Voters' Recognition of, and Support for Candidates in the Early Stages of a Campaign Period

It is important to grasp voters' characteristics in a district before making a campaign plan. The following table illustrates how to understand voters'

---

[21] Campaigns and Elections, August, 1998, 25.

characteristics by comparing voters' recognition of, and support for a candidate in a district.

Table 11.5 Analysis of voters' characteristics

	Low support	High support
High recognition	A	B
Low recognition	C	D

① Cell A in Table 11.5 shows that voters' recognition of candidates is high, but their support for the candidates is low in a district. This means that voters are interested in elections, but cannot find a candidate they would like to support. If a new candidate with a good record comes forward in this district, he/she may have a high chance of success.

② Cell B shows that both voters' recognition of, and support for candidates are high in a district. This means that voters are interested in elections and also have already found a candidate they would like to support. In this district, a new candidate would have a low chance of winning.

③ Cell C shows that both voters' recognition of, and support for candidates are low in a district. This purports that voters are little interested in elections and will not make much effort to get to know the candidates. In this district, a popular candidate may have a high chance of success, while a new and poorly known figure would have difficulty in winning.

④ Cell D shows that voters' recognition of candidates is low, but their support for candidates is high in a district. This means that most voters in this district are *straight-ticket voters*, who support a candidate because they like the political party nominating that candidate, rather than being impressed by the candidate's image and career. Therefore, in this district the candidate nominated by a major party would have a high chance of winning.

2. Analysis of Election Surveys

There are many ways to analyze election surveys. The following are those most frequently used ones.

(1) Analysis of Change in Support Caused by Change in the Number of the Main Candidates

It is very often seen that a new and popular candidate suddenly announces his/her candidacy in a district. In this case, candidates who have already announced their candidacy must know how the new candidate influences supporters for each of the candidates and undecided voters.

(a) Hypothetical Example in which the Frontrunner Gets a Blow

As indicated in Table 11.6, in the case in which both Candidates A and B have announced their candidacy 6 months before the election and Candidate C announces his/her candidacy two months before the election, Candidate C influences supporters for Candidates A and B. Before the announcement of Candidate C's candidacy, Candidate A is behind Candidate B by 10% in support.

However, after Candidate C's announcing his/her candidacy, support for the three candidates becomes almost the same.

Table 11.6 Support for two candidates versus for three candidates

	Support for Candidate A	Support for Candidate B	Support for Candidate C	Undecided voter
Two candidates	30%	40%	-	30%
Three candidates	26%	26%	24%	24%

In detail, support for Candidates A and B is 30% and 40% each, when the competition is only between the two of them. After Candidate C joins the competition, support for Candidates A and B becomes the same at 26%. Support for Candidates A and B is reduced by 4% and 14%, each. Support for Candidate C is 24%, thus equalizing the support for each of the three candidates.

Table 11.7 Support under changeover from two to three candidates

		Three candidates (A, B, C)			
		Support for A	Support for B	Support for C	Undecided voter
Two candidates (A, B)	Support for A	80%	0%	20%	0%
	Support for B	0%	60%	40%	0%
	Undecided voter	0%	0%	30%	70%

As indicated in Table 11.7, Candidate C stole 20% of the supporters for Candidate A, 40% of the supporters for Candidate B, and 30% of the undecided voters, when only Candidates A and B were running. This means that supporters of Candidate B are more similar to those of Candidate C than those of Candidate A in important characteristics. Therefore, the opponent whom Candidate B must criticize to raise support for him/herself is Candidate C.

(b) Hypothetical Example in which the Frontrunner Maintains a Superior position

Table 11.8 shows the results of an election survey. As indicated in the table, while Candidates A, B, and C have announced their candidacy a year before the election, Candidate D abruptly proclaims two months before the election that he/she is going to run.

After Candidate D joins the competition, support for Candidates A, B, and

C is reduced by 3.6%, 2.7% and 1.6%, respectively. Meanwhile, the number of undecided voters is curtailed by 6.4%. From this, we can interpret that Candidate D caused the greatest damage to Candidate A.

Table 11.8 Support for three versus four candidates

	Support for A	Support for B	Support for C	Support for D	Undecided voter
Three candidates	39.5%	25%	19.4%	-	16.1%
Four candidates	35.9%	22.3%	17.8%	14.3%	9.7%

However, in fact, Candidate D's candidacy only increases Candidate A's winning probability for the following reasons, as shown in Table 11.9.

Table 11.9 Support under changeover from three to four candidates

		Four candidates (A, B, C, D)				
		Support for A	Support for B	Support for C	Support for D	Undecided voter
Three candidates (A, B, C)	Support for A	83.8%	0.5%	1.5%	12.2%	2%
	Support for B	1.6%	86.5%	0.8%	11.1%	0%
	Support for C	0%	2.6%	85%	10%	12.4%
	Undecided voter	0%	0%	0%	39%	61%

① As indicated in Table 11.9, Candidate D steals 12.2% of the supporters for Candidate A, 11.1% of the supporters for Candidate B, and 10% of the supporters for Candidate C under competition among Candidates A, B and C. Since Candidate D steals votes from the other three candidates in a similar ratio, Candidate D's candidacy does not have a bad impact on Candidate A.

② Because Candidate D absorbs 39% of the undecided voters under competition among Candidates A, B and C, any of the Candidates B, C, or D cannot not win over Candidate A, although he/she draws all of the remaining undecided voters. This means that Candidate D's abrupt candidacy only consolidates Candidate A's victory. Candidate A does not need to do any active campaigning. In fact, some candidates in Korea induce the others, who have similar characteristics as their opponent, to announce their candidacy and win the election without much campaigning.

(2) Method to Measure the Effectiveness of a Campaign

It is very important to know how well a campaign is running during a campaign period. For this, the following questions are generally asked to respondents in the tracking surveys: *"Which candidate is superior in campaign activities?," "Which candidate is better at raising voters' recognition of, and support for him/herself?"* and *"Do a candidate and his/her canvassers work hard?"*

In the following, the method to examine the effectiveness of a campaign is described under the assumption that only campaign activities have an effect on candidate support, and all candidates are very similar to each other in all other respects, including voters' recognition of, and support for each of them, as well as the number of canvassers available.

Table 11.10 Method to measure the effectiveness of a campaign

		Voters' recognition of, and support for a candidate	
		High extent of rise	Low extent of rise
Campaign activities	Superior	A	C
	Inferior	B	D

① Cell A of Table 11.10 shows that a candidate is superior to his/her opponents in campaign activities, and voters' recognition of, and support for him/herself rise faster than in the case of his/her opponents. This implies that the candidate's campaign plan is sound, and the candidate and his/her canvassers are working hard.

② Cell B shows that a candidate is inferior to his/her opponents in campaign activities, but voters' recognition of, and support for him/herself rise faster than in the case of his/her opponents. This implies that his/her opponents' campaign is poorly planned and managed and/or his/her opponents and their canvassers are not working very hard.

③ Cell C shows that a candidate is superior to his/her opponents in campaign activities, but voters' recognition of, and support for him/herself do not rise faster than in the case of his/her opponents. This implies that the candidate and his/her canvassers are working hard but his/her campaign is poorly planned and managed.

④ Cell D shows that a candidate is inferior to his/her opponents in campaign activities, and voters' recognition of, and support for him/herself do not rise faster than in the case of his/her opponents. This implies that the candidate's campaign is poorly planned and managed and furthermore, that the candidate and his/her canvassers are not working hard.

(3) Method to Discriminate *Straight-Ticket Voters from Split-Ticket Voters*

Straight-ticket voters are usually those who support a candidate because they like the political party nominating the candidate, regardless of the candidate's image and career. *Straight-ticket voters* in the United States usually have a long-time psychological attachment to a certain party (called "party identification"). *Straight-ticket voters* in Korea are closely related to regionalism. More specifically, *straight-ticket voters* in Korea tend to support the candidate nominated by a certain party, because the voters are from the same region as the leader of that political party. Therefore, *straight-ticket voters'* intensity of support for a certain party is considerably high and stable, and it is difficult for a candidate to steal votes from *straight-ticket voters* supporting his/her opponent. This is why both in the United States and Korea, as well as in many other democratic countries, it is difficult to make *straight-ticket voters* the targets of a campaign.

Split-ticket voters are usually those who support a candidate on the basis of their evaluation of the candidate's career and record of performance. Their evaluation of a candidate's career and record of performance is easily changeable, and their intensity of support for a certain candidate is usually low and unstable. Therefore, they are apt to become the targets of a campaign.

The number of *straight-ticket voters* and *split-ticket voters* must be estimated in a district to make an appropriate campaign plan. The following method can be used to differentiate between *straight-ticket voters* and *split-ticket voters*.

Questions 1 and 2 are asked to estimate the number of *split-ticket voters* for Candidate M and *straight-ticket voters* for Party A. Candidate N must be someone who does not exist or is little known.

Q1) *"If Candidate M from Party A and Candidate P from Party B run for the upcoming election, whom will you support?"*

(1) *Candidate M of Party A*   (2) *Candidate P of Party B*   (3) *Don't know*

Q2) *"If Candidate N from Party A and Candidate P from Party B run for the upcoming election, whom will you support?"*

(1) *Candidate N of Party A*   (2) *Candidate P of Party B*   (3) *Don't know*

Straight-ticket voters for Party A are those who respond that they will support Party A in both Questions 1 and 2. That is, they are the ones supporting Party A, regardless of who the candidate of Party A is.

Meanwhile, respondents who answer that they support Candidate M of Party A in Question 1 and answer that they support Candidate P of Party B or answer *"Don't know"* in Question 2 are *split-ticket voters* supporting for Candidate M.

(4) Method to Discriminate *Fixed Supporters* from *Fluid Supporters*

Fixed supporters are those who very strongly support a certain candidate because they favor the candidate's party or the candidate's image or career.

Fluid supporters are those who are favorable to a certain candidate because they like the candidate's party or the candidate's image or career. However, they can switch and support other candidates if the situation changes. Question 3 is asked to estimate the number of *fixed supporters* for Candidate M.

Q3) *"Will you continue to support Candidate M or not, if there is a situation that makes you disappointed in Candidate M or his/her party?"*

(1) *Will continue to support Candidate M regardless of changes in the situation*

(2) *Can switch and support another candidate if the situation changes*

Fixed supporters for Candidate M are voters who will continue to support Candidate M, regardless of changes in the situation. *Fluid supporters* for Candidate M are voters who can switch and support another candidate if the situation changes.

Chapter 12
Four Factors Required for a Successful Campaign Strategist

This book has described various factors necessary for effectively planning and implementing campaign strategies. A campaign strategist can play a significant role in combining these factors to plan and implement campaign strategies, if they know theories concerning campaign strategies, have experience in serving in a campaign, have the capacity to collect and analyze information, and are men of ingenuity, as shown in Figure 12.1.

Figure 12.1 Four factors required for a successful campaign strategist

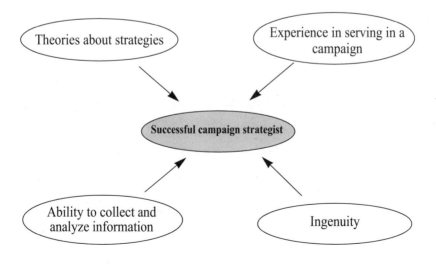

1. Theories about Campaign Strategies

Theories are made based on the accumulation of information obtained from past elections and they tell us what happened under certain conditions in past elections. These theories allow us to predict what may occur under similar conditions in an upcoming election. For instance, if a big political corruption is discovered during the campaign period, this incident can influence an election in three ways.

① The voting rate may decrease because voters will feel jaded about politics more than before the incident.

② The lower voting rate may be disadvantageous to candidates who have more weak supporters than their opponents. The reason is that weak supporters tend not to go to the voting booth under a disappointing political situation, while strong supporters are likely to vote under any political situation.

③ The incident may be advantageous to novice candidates rather than career candidates, because it may raise voters' disappointment with career candidates.

2. Experience in Serving in a Campaign

Since theories concerning campaign strategies are made based on only visible incidents that take place in the electoral process, small details that occur during the process of a campaign are not covered well by theories. For example, it may not be correct to say that anyone can communicate orally to other voters for the benefit of a certain candidate. Oral communication for the candidates by their canvasser, whom voters do not trust, would lead voters to think negatively about the candidate rather than positively. Such facts cannot be easily obtained from theories, but only from experience.

3. Ability to Collect and Analyze Information

Scientific campaign strategies are based on collecting and accurately analyzing information. Therefore, a campaign strategist must have the capacity to collect and analyze necessary information. For example, candidates make speeches a number of times in front of various voters during the campaign period. In order for a candidate's addresses to be effective, a campaign strategist must collect and analyze what kinds of topics a certain kind of voter would be interested in.

4. Ingenuity

Campaign environments are so complex that they sometimes cannot be covered by theories and experience. In this case, campaign strategists must be ingenious enough to create new strategies appropriate to the new environment.

For example, if the candidate that a campaign strategist is helping is a lot less known than his/her opponents, but looks very similar to a popular actor, the campaign strategist should suggest that the candidate use the actor's image to rapidly increase voters' recognition of him/herself.

Reference

Asher, Herbert. *Polling and the Public* (Washington, D.C.: Congressional
　　Quarterly Inc., 1992).
Campaigns & Elections (August, 1998).
Campaigns & Elections. *The Road to Victory* (Dubuque, Iowa, 1995).
Campbell, Angus. *American Voters* (Chicago: Midway, 1980).
The Headquater for Candidate Soon Cho, *For the New Election Culture*
　　(Seoul: Hakmin, 1995).
Esaiassion, Peter. "120 Years of Swedish Election Campaigns: A Story of the
　　Rise and Decline of Political Parties and the Emergence of the Mass
　　Media as Power Brokers," *Scandinavian Political Studies*, Vol.14, No.3.
Fleischman, Doris and Howard Cutler. "Themes and Symbols," in Bernays
　　Edward(ed.), *The Engineering of Consent* (Norman, Oklahoma:
　　Oklahoma University Press, 1955).
Hoffman, David and Ann Devroy. "The Complex Machine Behind Bush," in
　　Wayne Stephen and Cox Clyde, *Quest for National Office* (New York:
　　St. Martin's Press, 1992).
Kim, Young-Moon. *New Campaign Strategies* (Seoul: Hanoul, 1987).
Kim, Hak-Ryang. "A Study about the Ineffectiveness of Campaign
　　Organizations for the Parliamentary Election in Korea," East Asia
　　Institute in Kyung Nam University, *Far Eastern Studies*, Vol. 7, No.1.
　　――― . "The Impact of Unexpected Variables on Voting Behaviors," *Korean
　　Journal of Policy Analysis Evaluation*, Vol. 7, No. 1.
　　――― . Campaign Strategies (Seoul:Munwon, 1996).
Korea Gallup. *General Surveys*: 1992-1997 (Seoul: Korea Gallup, 1997).
No, Kyu-Hyung and Hak-Ryang Kim. "Studies about Effectiveness of
　　Campaign Strategies," a paper reported in the monthly conference of the

Korean Political Science Association, August, 1997.

Park, Kyung-Wook. *PR, PR* (Seoul: Ingansarang, 1994).

Park, Jong-Ryeal. *Politcal Advertisement and Campaign Strategies* (Seoul: Choinglim, 1987).

Ropper, William. *Winning Politics* (Randor, Pennsylvania: Chilton, 1978).

Song, Kun-Won and Hak-Rayng Kim. "What are Campaign Strategies" in *Election Korea*, Vol. 3.

Salmore, Barbara and Stephen Salmore. *Candidates, Parties, and Campaigns* (Washington, D.C.: Congressional Quarterly Inc., 1989).

Soruaf, Frank and Paul Beck. *Party Politics in America* (Boston: Scott, Foresman and Company, 1988).

The Conservative Party. *A Better Tomorrow*(1970).

The League of Women Voters of California Education Fund. *Choosing the President* (New York: Lyons & Burford, 1992).

Tor, Bj ø klund. "Election Campaigns in Postwar Norway 1945-1989: From Party-Controlled to Media-Driven Campaigns," *Scandinavian Political Studies*, Vol.14, No.3.

Trent, Judith and Robert Fridenberg. *Political Campaign Communication* (New York: Praeger, 1991).

INDEX